THE
POWER
OF
MOMENTS

www.**penguin**.co.uk

THE
POWER
OF
MOMENTS

Why Certain Experiences
Have Extraordinary Impact

CHIP AND DAN HEATH

BANTAM PRESS

LONDON • TORONTO • SYDNEY • AUCKLAND • JOHANNESBURG

TRANSWORLD PUBLISHERS
61–63 Uxbridge Road, London W5 5SA
www.penguin.co.uk

Transworld is part of the Penguin Random House group of companies
whose addresses can be found at global.penguinrandomhouse.com

Penguin
Random House
UK

First published in Great Britain in 2017 by Bantam Press
an imprint of Transworld Publishers

A CIP catalogue record for this book
is available from the British Library.

ISBN 9780593079263

Typeset in Electra
Printed and bound by Clays Ltd, Bungay, Suffolk.

Penguin Random House is committed to a sustainable
future for our business, our readers and our planet. This book
is made from Forest Stewardship Council® certified paper.

MIX
Paper from
responsible sources
FSC® C018179

To our daughters Emory, Aubrey, and Josephine,
whose defining moments become ours

Contents

1

Defining Moments

1.

Chris Barbic and Donald Kamentz were sitting at a pub in Houston, recuperating from another 14-hour day running their start-up charter school. They were drinking beer. Watching ESPN. And sharing a Tombstone pizza, the bar's only food offering. They had no idea, on that night in October 2000, that they were moments away from an epiphany that would affect thousands of lives.

ESPN was covering National Signing Day, the first day when graduating high school football players can sign a binding "letter of intent" to attend a particular college. For college football fans, it's a big day.

Watching the exuberant coverage, something struck Kamentz. "It blows my mind that we celebrate athletics this way, but we don't have anything that celebrates academics in the same way," he said. And the students at their school—primarily kids from low-income Hispanic families—deserved celebrating. Many of them would be the first in their families to graduate from high school.

Barbic had founded a school to serve those students. He'd grown disillusioned teaching sixth grade at a local elementary school. "I saw way too many of my students head off to the local junior high excited about school and eager to pursue their dreams, only to return a few months later with that light in their eyes totally gone." They would come back to visit him, telling stories of gangs, drugs, pregnancies. It crushed him. He knew he had two choices: Quit teaching to spare himself. Or build the school that those students deserved. So in 1998, Barbic founded YES Prep. And Donald Kamentz was one of the first people he hired.

In the pub that night, as they watched the Signing Day news, they had a sudden inspiration: *What if we created our own "Signing Day," when our students would announce where they will attend college?* The event would allow them to honor all graduating seniors, since it was a condition of graduation at YES Prep that every student apply and be accepted to college, even if they ultimately chose not to attend.

Their excitement grew as they shaped the idea: They would call it Senior Signing Day, and for that one day, graduating seniors would be treated with the same hype and adulation as college athletes.

About six months later, on April 30, 2001, they held the first Senior Signing Day. Roughly 450 people crammed into a community center next door to their campus: 17 graduating seniors and their families, along with every other student in the YES Prep system—from juniors to sixth graders.

Each of the seniors took the stage, announcing where he or she would be attending college in the fall: "My name is Eddie Zapata, and in the fall, I will be attending Vanderbilt University!" They would unveil a T-shirt or pennant with their chosen school's insignia. Many of the students kept their final school decision a secret from friends, so there was suspense in the air. After each announcement, the room erupted with cheers.

Later, the students would sit at a table, with their families crowded around them, and sign letters of matriculation, confirming their enrollment in the fall. Barbic was struck by the emotion of the "signing" moment: "It hits home—the sacrifices that everybody had to make for their kids to get there. No one did it alone. There were lots of people involved." By the end of the ceremony, there were few dry eyes in the room.

Senior Signing Day became the most important annual event for the YES Prep school network. For seniors, the event was a celebration, the capstone of their achievement. But it held a different kind of meaning for younger students. At the third Senior Signing Day, which had expanded into an auditorium at the University of Houston, there was a sixth grader in the audience named Mayra Valle. It was her first Signing Day experience, and it made a lasting impression. She remembers thinking, *That could be me. No one in my family has ever gone to college. I want to be on that stage.*

By 2010, six years later, the senior class had grown to 126

graduates, and Signing Day had expanded so much that it had moved to the basketball arena at Rice University, in front of 5,000 people. 90% of the graduates that year were the first members of their families to go to college.

The keynote speaker, U.S. secretary of education Arne Duncan, was moved by what he saw. He scrapped his prepared remarks and spoke freely: "No basketball game, no football game begins to compare to the magnitude and importance of what happened here today. . . . Thank you for inspiring not just your brothers and sisters, not just the underclassmen here, but the entire country."

One of the graduating seniors was Mayra Valle. Six years after she imagined being on that stage, today was her day. "Good afternoon, everybody, my name is Mayra Valle," she said, breaking into an enormous smile. "And this fall I will be attending CONNECTICUT COLLEGE!" The school was ranked one of the top 50 liberal arts colleges in the country.

The crowd roared.

2.

We all have defining moments in our lives—meaningful experiences that stand out in our memory. Many of them owe a great deal to chance: A lucky encounter with someone who becomes the love of your life. A new teacher who spots a talent you didn't know you had. A sudden loss that upends the certainties of your life. A realization that you don't want to spend one more day in your job. These moments seem to be the product of fate or luck or maybe a higher power's interventions. We can't control them.

But is that true? Must our defining moments *just happen to us?*

Senior Signing Day didn't just happen. Chris Barbic and Donald Kamentz set out to *create* a defining moment for their students. When Mayra Valle and hundreds of other YES Prep graduates walked onto that stage, they stepped into a carefully crafted defining moment that was no less special for having been planned. It's a moment they'll never forget.

Defining moments shape our lives, but we don't have to wait for them to happen. We can be the authors of them. What if a teacher could design a lesson that students were still reflecting on years later? What if a manager knew exactly how to turn an employee's moment of failure into a moment of growth? What if you had a better sense of how to create lasting memories for your kids?

In this book, we have two goals: First, we want to examine defining moments and identify the traits they have in common. What, specifically, makes a particular experience memorable and meaningful? Our research shows that defining moments share a set of common elements.

Second, we want to show you how you can *create* defining moments by making use of those elements. Why would you want to create them? To enrich your life. To connect with others. To make memories. To improve the experience of customers or patients or employees.

Our lives are measured in moments, and defining moments

are the ones that endure in our memories. In the pages ahead, we'll show you how to make more of them.

3.

Why do we remember certain experiences and forget others? In the case of Signing Day, the answer is pretty clear: It's a celebration that is grand in scale and rich in emotion. No surprise that it's more memorable than a lesson on multiplying fractions. But for other experiences in life—from vacations to work projects—it's not as clear why we remember what we do.

Psychologists have discovered some counterintuitive answers to this puzzle of memory. Let's say you take your family to Disney World. During your visit, we text you every hour, asking you to rate your experience at that moment on a scale from 1 to 10, where 1 is lousy and 10 is terrific. Let's assume we check in with you 6 times. Here's how your day shapes up:

> **9 a.m.:** Cattle-herding your kids out of the hotel room. There's excitement in the air. Rating: 6
>
> **10 a.m.:** Riding "It's a Small World" together, with parents and children each under the impression that the other must be enjoying this. Rating: 5
>
> **11 a.m.:** Feeling a dopamine rush after riding the Space Mountain roller coaster. Your kids are begging to ride it again. Rating: 10
>
> **Noon:** Enjoying expensive park food with your kids, who

might enjoy it less if they knew you bought it with
their college fund. Rating: 7

1 p.m.: Waiting in line, for 45 minutes now, in the
96-degree central Florida heat. Trying to keep your
son from gnawing on the handrails. Rating: 3

2 p.m.: Buying mouse-ear hats on the way out of the
park. Your kids look so cute. Rating: 8

To arrive at an overall summary of your day, we could simply average those ratings: 6.5. A pretty good day.

Now, let's say we text you again, a few weeks later, and ask you to rate your *overall* Disney experience. A reasonable prediction of your answer would be 6.5, since it encompasses all the highs and lows of your day.

But psychologists would say that's way off. They'd predict that, looking back on the day at Disney, your overall rating would be a 9! That's because research has found that in recalling an experience, we ignore most of what happened and focus instead on a few particular moments. Specifically, two moments will stand out: riding Space Mountain and buying mouse-ear hats. To understand why those two moments matter more than the others, let's explore some of the underlying psychology.

Consider an experiment in which participants were asked to undergo three painful trials. In the first, they submerged their hands for 60 seconds in buckets filled with frigid, 57-degree water. (Keep in mind that 57-degree water feels *much* colder than 57-degree air.)

The second trial was similar, except that they kept their

hands submerged for 90 seconds instead of 60, and during the final 30 seconds, the water warmed up to 59 degrees. That final half minute was still unpleasant, but noticeably less so for most participants. (Note that the researchers were monitoring the time carefully, but the participants were not told how much time had elapsed.)

For their third painful experience, the participants were given a choice: Would you rather repeat the first trial or the second?

This is an easy question: Both trials featured 60 seconds of identical pain, and the second trial added another 30 seconds of slightly reduced pain. So this is kind of like asking, *Would you rather be slapped in the face for 60 seconds or 90?*

Nevertheless, 69% chose the longer trial.

Psychologists have untangled the reasons for this puzzling result. When people assess an experience, they tend to forget or ignore its length—a phenomenon called "duration neglect." Instead, they seem to rate the experience based on two key moments: (1) the best or worst moment, known as the "peak"; and (2) the ending. Psychologists call it the "peak-end rule."

So in the participants' memories, the difference between 60 and 90 seconds washed out. That's duration neglect. And what stood out for them was that the longer trial *ended more comfortably* than the shorter one. (Both trials, by the way, had a similar peak moment of pain: close to the 60-second mark.)

This research explains why, in reflecting on your Disney experience, you'll remember Space Mountain (the peak) and the mouse ears (the end). Everything else will tend to fade. As a result, your memory of the day is far more favorable than the hour-by-hour ratings you provided.

The peak-end rule holds true across many kinds of experiences. Most of the relevant studies tend to focus on short, laboratory-friendly experiences: watching film clips, enduring annoying sounds, etc. On longer time frames, peaks continue to matter but the relative importance of "endings" fades somewhat. Beginnings matter, too: When college alumni were asked about their memories from college, fully 40% of those memories came from the month of September! And beginnings and endings can blur—if you change cities for a new job, is that an ending or a beginning or both? That's why it's preferable to talk about *transitions*, which encompass both endings and beginnings.

What's indisputable is that when we assess our experiences, we don't average our minute-by-minute sensations. Rather, we tend to remember flagship moments: the peaks, the pits, and the transitions.

This is a critical lesson for anyone in service businesses— from restaurants to medical clinics to call centers to spas— where success hinges on the customer experience. Consider the Magic Castle Hotel, which as of press time was one of the three top-rated hotels in Los Angeles, out of hundreds. It triumphed over competition like the Four Seasons Hotel at Beverly Hills and the Ritz-Carlton Los Angeles. Magic Castle's reviews are stunning: Out of more than 2,900 reviews on TripAdvisor, over 93% of guests rate the hotel as either "excellent" or "very good."

There's something odd about the hotel's ranking, though: If

you flipped through the photos of the resort online, you would never conclude, "That's one of the best hotels in L.A." An interior courtyard features a pool that might qualify as Olympic size, if the Olympics were being held in your backyard. The rooms are dated, the furnishings are spare, and most walls are bare. In fact, even the word *hotel* seems like a stretch—the Magic Castle is actually a converted two-story apartment complex from the 1950s, painted canary yellow.

The point is not that it's a bad-looking place; it's fine. It looks like a respectable budget motel. But the Four Seasons it ain't. Nor is it particularly cheap—the pricing is comparable to Hilton or Marriott hotels. How could it be one of the top-rated hotels in Los Angeles?

Let's start with the cherry-red phone mounted to a wall near the pool. You pick it up and someone answers, "Hello, Popsicle Hotline." You place an order, and minutes later, a staffer wearing white gloves delivers your cherry, orange, or grape Popsicles to you at poolside. On a silver tray. For free.

Then there's the Snack Menu, a list of goodies—ranging from Kit-Kats to root beer to Cheetos—that can be ordered up at no cost. There's also a Board Game Menu and a DVD Menu, with all items loaned for free. Three times a week, magicians perform tricks at breakfast. Did we mention you can drop off unlimited loads of laundry for free washing? Your clothes are returned later in the day, wrapped in butcher paper and tied up with twine and a sprig of lavender. Which is much more pomp and ceremony than the doctor used when handing off your first child.

The guest reviews for the Magic Castle Hotel are rapturous. What the Magic Castle has figured out is that, to please customers, you need not obsess over every detail. Customers will forgive small swimming pools and underwhelming room décor, as long as some moments are magical. The surprise about great service experiences is that they are *mostly forgettable and occasionally remarkable.*

Now, when you phone the "Popsicle Hotline," is that a defining moment? In the context of a lifetime, certainly not. (Hard to imagine a deathbed regret: "If only I'd chosen the grape . . .")

But in the context of a vacation? Of course it's a defining moment. When tourists tell their friends about their vacation to Southern California, they'll say, "We went to Disneyland, and we saw the Walk of Fame, and we stayed at this hotel, the Magic Castle, and you won't believe this, but there's a phone by the pool . . ." The Popsicle Hotline is one of the moments that defines the trip. And it was an engineered moment—the kind of moment that other hotels fail to conjure. (Courtyards by Marriott are fine places, but can you imagine *raving* about them to a friend?)

The point here is simple: Some moments are vastly more meaningful than others. For tourists, the Popsicle Hotline is a 15-minute experience that pops out of the surrounding 2-week vacation. For students at YES Prep, Senior Signing Day is a single morning that rises above a 7-year journey.

But we tend to ignore this truth. We're not very good at *investing* in such moments. For example, a teacher plans his history curriculum for a semester, but every class period gets roughly the same amount of attention. There's no attempt to shape a few "peak" moments. Or an executive leads her company through a fast-growth period, but there's little to distinguish one week from the next. Or we spend weekend after weekend together with our kids, but in memory all those times blend together.

How can we fight this flatness and make moments that matter? Let's start with the basics: How are we defining a "defining moment"? In common usage, the term is applied in a variety of ways. Some use it to capture dramatic times when people have their character tested, as with a soldier showing courage in battle. Others use the term more liberally, as almost a synonym for "greatest hits." (For example, an online search of the term yields results such as "Defining Moments in 70s Television," which must have been a short list indeed.)

For the sake of this book, a defining moment is a short experience that is both memorable and meaningful. ("Short" is relative here—a month might be a short experience in the span of your life, and a minute might be short in the context of a customer support call.) There may be a dozen moments in your life that capture who you are—those are big defining moments. But there are smaller experiences, such as the Popsicle Hotline, that are defining moments in the context of a vacation or a semester abroad or a product development cycle.

What are these moments made of, and how do we create more of them? In our research, we have found that defining moments are created from one or more of the following four elements:

ELEVATION: Defining moments rise above the everyday. They provoke not just transient happiness, like laughing at a friend's joke, but memorable delight. (You pick up the red phone and someone says, "Popsicle Hotline, we'll be right out.") To construct elevated moments, we must boost sensory pleasures—the Popsicles must be delivered poolside on a silver tray, of course—and, if appropriate, add an element of surprise. We'll see why surprise can warp our perceptions of time, and why most people's most memorable experiences are clustered in their teens and twenties. Moments of elevation transcend the normal course of events; they are literally extraordinary.

INSIGHT: Defining moments rewire our understanding of ourselves or the world. In a few seconds or minutes, we realize something that might influence our lives for decades: *Now is the time for me to start this business.* Or, *This is the person I'm going to marry.* The psychologist Roy Baumeister studied life changes that were precipitated by a "crystallization of discontent," moments when people abruptly saw things as they were, such as cult members who suddenly realized the truth about their leader. And although these moments of insight often seem serendipitous, we can engineer them—or at the very least, lay the groundwork. In one unforgettably disgusting story, we'll see how some relief workers sparked social change by causing a community to "trip over the truth."

PRIDE: Defining moments capture us at our best—moments of achievement, moments of courage. To create such moments, we need to understand something about the architecture of pride—how to plan for a series of milestone moments that build on each other en route to a larger goal. We'll explore why the "Couch to 5K" program was so successful—and so much more effective in sparking exercise than the simple imperative to "jog more." And we'll learn some unexpected things about acts of courage and the surprising ripple effects they create.

CONNECTION: Defining moments are social: weddings, graduations, baptisms, vacations, work triumphs, bar and bat mitzvahs, speeches, sporting events. These moments are strengthened because we share them with others. What triggers moments of connection? We'll encounter a remarkable laboratory procedure that allows two people to walk into a room as strangers and walk out, 45 minutes later, as close friends. And we'll analyze what one social scientist believes is a kind of unified theory of what makes relationships stronger, whether the bond is between husband and wife, doctor and patient, or even shopper and retailer.

Defining moments often spark positive emotion—we'll use "positive defining moments" and "peaks" interchangeably throughout the book—but there are categories of *negative* defining moments, too, such as moments of pique: experiences of embarrassment or embitterment that cause people to vow, "I'll show them!" There's another category that is all too common: moments of trauma, which leave us heartbroken and grieving. In the pages ahead, we'll encounter several stories of people dealing with trauma, but we will not explore this category in detail, for the simple reason that our focus is on creating more positive moments. No one wants to experience more moments of loss. In the Appendix, we share some resources that people who have suffered a trauma might find helpful.

Defining moments possess at least one of the four elements above, but they need not have all four. Many moments of insight, for example, are private—they don't involve a connection. And a fun moment like calling the Popsicle Hotline doesn't offer much insight or pride.

Some powerful defining moments contain all four elements. Think of YES Prep's Senior Signing Day: the ELEVATION of students having their moment onstage, the INSIGHT of a sixth grader thinking *That could be me*, the PRIDE of being accepted to college, and the CONNECTION of sharing the day with an arena full of thousands of supportive people. (See the footnote for a mnemonic to remember this framework for defining moments.)*

Sometimes these elements can be very personal. Somewhere in your home there is a treasure chest, full of things that are precious to you and worthless to anyone else. It might be a scrapbook, or a drawer in a dresser, or a box in the attic. Maybe some of your favorites are stuck on the refrigerator so you can see them every day. Wherever your treasure chest is, its contents are likely to include the four elements we've been discussing:

---

* It may not have escaped your attention that if you swap the order of Insight and Pride, you get a handy acronym: EPIC. We have mixed feelings about this. An acronym, in a book like this, boosts memorability at the cost of some cheesiness. In the past, we have happily embraced that trade, having used two acronyms in previous books to help people recall the relevant frameworks. In this case, we have decided against it. For one thing, we're not advising you to pursue "epic" moments. Some of the stories you'll encounter do fit that description, but many others are small and personal, or painful but transformational. *Epic* seems too grandiose and too shallow all at once. Also, and this is a personal failing, we can't read the word *epic* without imagining it being spoken by a stoned surfer dude. (You see what we mean now, don't you?) So, bottom line, if the EPIC acronym helps you remember the four elements, please keep it with our compliments. But this is the last time we'll mention it.

- **ELEVATION:** A love letter. A ticket stub. A well-worn T-shirt. Haphazardly colored cards from your kids that make you smile with delight.
- **INSIGHT:** Quotes or articles that moved you. Books that changed your view of the world. Diaries that captured your thoughts.
- **PRIDE:** Ribbons, report cards, notes of recognition, certificates, thank-yous, awards. (It just *hurts*, irrationally, to throw away a trophy.)
- **CONNECTION:** Wedding photos. Vacation photos. Family photos. Christmas photos of hideous sweaters. Lots of photos. Probably the first thing you'd grab if your house caught on fire.

All these items you're safeguarding are, in essence, the relics of your life's defining moments. How are you feeling now as you reflect on the contents of your treasure chest? What if you could give that same feeling to your kids, your students, your colleagues, your customers?

Moments matter. And what an opportunity we miss when we leave them to chance! Teachers can inspire, caregivers can comfort, service workers can delight, politicians can unite, and managers can motivate. All it takes is a bit of insight and forethought.

This is a book about the power of moments and the wisdom of shaping them.

2

Thinking in Moments

1.

What was your first day like at your current (or most recent) job?

Is it fair to say that it was *not* a defining moment?

Judging from the stories we've heard from underwhelmed employees, what follows is a pretty typical description of a first day: You show up. The receptionist didn't think you were starting until next week. You're shown to a desk. There's a monitor and an Ethernet cable on the desk but no computer. There's also a single binder clip. The chair still bears the imprint of the previous owner, like an ergonomic buttocks fossil.

Your boss has not arrived yet. You're given an ethics and compliance manual to review. "Why don't you read over this and I'll swing back in a few hours?" says the receptionist. The sexual harassment policy is so long and comprehensive it makes you wonder a bit about your colleagues.

Eventually, a friendly person from your floor introduces herself and whisks you around the office, interrupting 11 different people to introduce you. As a result, you worry that you have managed to annoy all of your colleagues within the first hour of your employment. You immediately forget all their names. Except Lester, who might just be the reason for the sexual harassment policy?

Does that sound about right?

The lack of attention paid to an employee's first day is mind-boggling. What a wasted opportunity to make a new team member feel included and appreciated. Imagine if you treated a first date like a new employee: "I've got some meetings stacked up right now, so why don't you get settled in the passenger seat of the car and I'll swing back in a few hours?"

To avoid this kind of oversight, we must understand when special moments are needed. We must learn to *think in moments,* to spot the occasions that are worthy of investment.

This "moment-spotting" habit can be unnatural. In organizations, for instance, we are consumed with goals. Time is meaningful only insofar as it clarifies or measures our goals. The goal is the thing.

But for an individual human being, moments are the thing. Moments are what we remember and what we cherish. Certainly we might celebrate achieving a goal, such as completing a marathon or landing a significant client—but the achievement is embedded in a moment.

Every culture has its prescribed set of big moments: birthdays and weddings and graduations, of course, but also holiday celebrations and funeral rites and political traditions. They seem "natural" to us. But notice that every last one of them was invented, dreamed up by anonymous authors who wanted to give shape to time. This is what we mean by "thinking in moments": to recognize where the prose of life needs punctuation.

We'll explore three situations that deserve punctuation: transitions, milestones, and pits. Transitions are classic occasions for defining moments. Many cultures have a "coming of age" ritual, like the bar and bat mitzvah or the quinceañera. In the Sateré-Mawé tribe in the Brazilian Amazon, when a boy turns 13, he comes of age by wearing a pair of gloves filled with angry, stinging bullet ants, leaving his hands covered in welts. Because someone apparently asked, "How can we make puberty harder?"

Coming-of-age rituals are boundary markers, attempts to crisp up an otherwise gradual evolution from adolescence to adulthood. *Before this day, I was a child. After this day, I am a man. (A man with very swollen hands.)*

Transitions, like milestones and pits, are *natural* defining moments. The transition of getting married is a defining moment in life regardless of whether it is celebrated. But if we recognize how important these natural defining moments are, we can shape them—make them more memorable and meaningful.

That logic shows why the first day of work is an experience worth investing in. For new employees, it's three big transitions at once: intellectual (new work), social (new people), and envi-

ronmental (new place). The first day shouldn't be a set of bu-
reaucratic activities on a checklist. It should be a peak moment.

Lani Lorenz Fry understood this opportunity. Fry, who worked
in global brand strategy and marketing at John Deere, had heard
from the company's leaders in Asia that they were struggling with
employee engagement and retention. "John Deere is not a well-
known brand there," Fry said. "It's not like the Midwest in the
U.S., where your grandpa probably had a John Deere tractor."
As a result, employees had less of an emotional tie to the brand.

Fry and her colleagues on the brand team saw an opportunity
to build that connection—and it had to start on the employee's
first day. Collaborating with the customer experience consultant
Lewis Carbone, the team designed what it called the First Day
Experience. Here's the way they wanted the day to unfold (you
may notice some differences from the first-day story above):

*Shortly after you accept the offer letter from John Deere,
you get an email from a John Deere Friend. Let's call
her Anika. She introduces herself and shares some of the
basics: where to park, what the dress norms are, and so
forth. She also tells you that she'll be waiting to greet
you in the lobby at 9 a.m. on your first day.*

*When your first day comes, you park in the right
place and make your way to the lobby, and there's
Anika! You recognize her from her photo. She points to
the flat-screen monitor in the lobby—it features a giant
headline: "Welcome, Arjun!"*

*Anika shows you to your cubicle. There's a six-foot-
tall banner set up next to it—it rises above the cubes to*

alert people that there's a new hire. People stop by over the course of the day to say hello to you.

As you get settled, you notice the background image on your monitor: It's a gorgeous shot of John Deere equipment on a farm at sunset, and the copy says, "Welcome to the most important work you'll ever do."

You notice you've already received your first email. It's from Sam Allen, the CEO of John Deere. In a short video, he talks a little bit about the company's mission: "to provide the food, shelter, and infrastructure that will be needed by the world's growing population." He closes by saying, "Enjoy the rest of your first day, and I hope you'll enjoy a long, successful, fulfilling career as part of the John Deere team."

Now you notice there's a gift on your desk. It's a stainless steel replica of John Deere's original "self-polishing plow," created in 1837. An accompanying card explains why farmers loved it.

At midday, Anika collects you for a lunch off-site with a small group. They ask about your background and tell you about some of the projects they're working on. Later in the day, the department manager (your boss's boss) comes over and makes plans to have lunch with you the next week.

You leave the office that day thinking, I belong here. The work we're doing matters. And I matter to them.

After the John Deere brand team completed its plan for the First Day Experience, some offices across Asia began to roll it out. In the Beijing office, it was such a hit that employees who'd been hired earlier were joking, "Can I quit and rejoin?" In India, the program has helped to differentiate John Deere in the highly competitive labor market.

Shouldn't every organization in the world have a version of this First Day Experience?

2.

John Deere's First Day Experience is a peak moment delivered at *a time of transition*. When a life transition lacks a "moment," though, it can become formless. We often feel anxious because we don't know how to act or what rules to apply. Consider a story shared by Kenneth Doka, a licensed mental health counselor who is also an expert on grief.

A woman came to him who had lost her husband to Lou Gehrig's disease (amyotrophic lateral sclerosis, or ALS). They'd had a happy marriage, she said. He was a good father and a good husband. But ALS is a cruel, degenerative disease, and as her husband's illness advanced, he required more and more care. It was tough for both of them. He was a proud man—the owner of a small construction firm—and "didn't do sick well," as she said. They fought more than they ever had.

But they were devout Catholics, and they had tremendous faith in their marriage. She said that every night, after a tough day, they'd put their hands together in bed so that their rings touched, and they'd repeat their wedding vows to each other.

When she came to see Doka, it had been six years since her husband passed, and she told him that she thought she was ready to start dating again. "But I can't take my wedding ring off," she said. "I can't date with my wedding ring, and I can't take it off." She believed that marriages were for life, but she also knew that she had honored her commitment. She was confused and stuck.

Doka has written extensively about the power of "therapeutic rituals" to help people who are grieving. He suggested that she needed a "ritual of transition" to take off the ring, and she liked the idea. So, with her permission, he worked with her priest to create a small ceremony.

It happened one Sunday afternoon, after Mass, in the church where she was married. The priest had called together a group of her close friends and family members, many of whom had attended her wedding.

The priest called them up around the altar. Then he began to ask her some questions.

"Were you faithful in good times and bad?"

"Yes," she said.

"In sickness and health?"

"Yes."

The priest led her through her wedding vows—but in the past tense. She affirmed, in the presence of the witnesses, that she had been faithful, that she had loved and honored her husband.

Then the priest said, "May I have the ring, please?" She took it off her finger and handed it to him. She would tell Doka later that "it came off as if by magic."

The priest accepted her ring. He and Doka had arranged for her ring to be interlocked with her husband's ring and then affixed to the front of their wedding photo.

The ceremony allowed her to attest, to herself and the people she loved, that she had fulfilled her vows. It signaled to everyone present that her identity was about to change. It was a moment that allowed her a fresh start.

At the heart of the "reverse wedding" story is a powerful insight. At the point the widow went to see Doka, she was ready to begin dating again. And it's clear that, even if she hadn't met Doka, she would have started dating eventually on her own. Maybe it would have taken a month, maybe a year, maybe five years. And throughout that uncertain time, she would have felt anxious: *Am I ready? Is it "okay" for me to be ready?* What the widow in Doka's story needed was a landmark moment to capture the transition she was making. *After that Sunday afternoon ceremony, I was ready.*

We have a natural hunger for these landmarks in time. Take the prevalence of New Year's resolutions. The Wharton professor Katherine Milkman said she found it striking that "at the start of a new year, we feel like we have a clean slate. It's the 'fresh start effect' . . . all of my past failures are from last year and I can think, 'Those are not me. That's old me. That's not new me. New me isn't going to make these mistakes.'"

In other words, New Year's resolutions are not really about the resolutions. After all, for most people, the resolutions haven't changed. Most people wanted to lose weight and save money on December 31, too. What we're doing on New Year's Day is more like a mental accounting trick. Our past failures are left on the ledger of Old Me. New Me starts today.

New Year's resolutions should really be called New Year's absolutions.

Milkman realized that if her "fresh start" theory was right, then the slate-cleaning effect shouldn't be confined to New Year's Day. It should also be true for other landmark dates that would give us an excuse to reset our record, such as the start of a new month or even a new week.

Milkman and her colleague Hengchen Dai tracked down attendance data for a university fitness center, and they found strong proof of their "fresh start" hypothesis. The probability that students visited the gym increased at the beginning of each new week (by 33%), new month (by 14%), and new semester (by 47%).

So "fresh starts" happen not only on New Year's Day, but also on any other landmark date. If you're struggling to make a transition, create a defining moment that draws a dividing line between Old You and New You.

3.

There are certain landmark dates that are near universal. A survey by the researchers Adam Alter and Hal Hershfield asked participants to specify the most significant birthdays across a person's life span. The winners (ranked in order of votes) were:

18
21
30

40

50

60

100

These are *milestone* birthdays, and every one of them calls for a celebration or, in the case of the 100th birthday, a grudging gratitude that the odometer is still moving. Other than 18 and 21, which come with an expansion of civic and alcoholic rights, respectively, these numbers are arbitrary. Turning 50 seems like a real threshold of some kind, but of course it's not. There is no day in your whole life when you are more than a day older than the day before (unless Daylight Savings is the black magic it seems to be). Aging is exquisitely incremental. To add meaning to our lives, though, we concoct these thresholds—30, 40, 50— and then freak out when we get close to them.

But being arbitrary doesn't make these occasions less meaningful. Milestones are milestones. And just as there are familiar defining moments that mark transitions, such as graduation ceremonies, there are others that commemorate milestones: 40th birthday parties. 25th anniversary trips. 30th-year-on-the-job plaques or gold watches.

We will not dwell on milestones, since people seem to have a natural knack for noticing them. But, as with moments of transition, there are some milestones that seem to go ignored. Students get short-changed, for instance. Sure, they advance in "grade," but why not celebrate their 1,000th day in the classroom, or their 50th book read? And why don't we celebrate teachers for their 1,000th student taught?

Companies in this era of apps and personal tracking devices have grown much smarter about surfacing milestones that were previously invisible. The app Pocket, which stores articles from the Internet on your phone for later reading, informs users when they've read 1 million words. The fitness-tracking bracelet Fitbit presents users with awards such as the 747 Badge, given for climbing 4,000 lifetime flights of stairs (which rises roughly to the altitude that 747s fly), and the Monarch Migration Badge, which is described as follows: "Every year the monarch butterfly migrates 2,500 miles to warmer climates. With the same lifetime miles in your pocket, you're giving those butterflies some hot competition!"

These companies are cleverly conjuring up defining moments of pride—for the trivial cost of an email. All it required was some attention to milestones.

4.

To think in moments is to be attuned to transitions and milestones as well as to a third type of experience: pits. Pits are the opposite of peaks. They are negative defining moments—moments of hardship or pain or anxiety.

Pits need to be *filled*. Most of the time, this is simply common sense. Disney knows, for example, that people hate long lines. So Disney invests in ways to fill that pit, by creating interesting displays as a distraction, and having performers interact with guests, and setting expectations about the wait. And in our personal lives, it's similarly obvious. You need not study a book on defining moments to understand that if your partner is suffering, you attend to them.

Yet as we've seen, common sense can have a limited range. Graduations are common sense; first-day-of-work experiences are not. 40th birthday parties are common sense; 1,000th-day-in-school parties aren't. And the same is true with pits. As a small example, take someone who leases a car and dies during the lease term. No doubt your common sense says that the deceased's family could simply return the car and discontinue the lease. Wrong. Rather than recognize an opportunity to perform a simple act of kindness in a difficult time, most car finance companies say: Pay up. Mercedes-Benz Financial Services, rare among its competitors, sends a condolence letter to the lessee's family with an offer to forgive the lease obligation.

Or consider patients who have just learned that they have cancer. Doctors and nurses know to be compassionate and supportive in those fraught moments. But comfort only goes so far; what about quick *action*? In many cases, patients must wait several weeks or more to begin seeing the chain of specialists who will treat them. Not at Intermountain Healthcare. As reported by Leonard Berry and two colleagues, the patient and his or her family are invited to a meeting within a week of the cancer diagnosis. They stay put in one room and the members of their caregiving team circulate in and out: surgeons, oncologists, dietitians, social workers, and nurses. The patients walk out at the end of the day with a comprehensive plan of care and a set of scheduled appointments. This is not to minimize the importance of giving comfort to a patient. Of course that's vital. It's simply to say that giving comfort is commonsensical. But scheduling a rapid, all-hands meeting to formulate a plan of attack—that's not common sense, that's a conscious effort to fill a pit.

What's least commonsensical is that pits can sometimes be flipped into peaks. A study of service encounters asked customers to recall recent satisfying and dissatisfying interactions with employees of airlines, hotels, or restaurants. Almost 25% of the positive encounters cited by customers were actually employees' responses to *service failures*: slow service, mistaken orders, lost reservations, delayed flights, and so on. When employees handled these situations well, they transformed a negative moment to a positive one. Every great service company is a master of service *recovery*. (An executive of a company that builds custom homes shared with us an insight from his customer satisfaction data. To maximize customer satisfaction, he said, you don't want to be perfect. You want to get two things wrong, have the customer bring those mistakes to your attention, and then hustle like mad to fix those problems. Thankfully, he hadn't instructed his team to start making mistakes on purpose. But we could tell he was tempted . . .)

Business leaders who can spot their customers' moments of dissatisfaction and vulnerability—and take decisive action to support those customers—will have no trouble differentiating themselves from competitors. Offering to help someone in a difficult time is its own goal and reward. It also has the side effect of being good for business.

Take the story of Doug Dietz, an industrial designer from General Electric. He'd spent two years working on a new MRI machine, and in the fall of 2007, he had his first chance to see the machine installed in a hospital. He said he felt like a "proud Papa" going to see his baby.

When he entered the MRI suite, he saw the new diagnostic imaging machine and "did a happy dance," he said in a 2012 TED Talk. Dietz retreated to the hall to watch for the first patients. While he waited, he saw a couple and their young daughter coming down the hallway. The girl was crying. As they got closer to the room, the father leaned down to the girl and said, "We've talked about this. You can be brave."

As soon as the little girl entered the room, she froze, terrified. And in that moment, Dietz could see the way the room looked through her eyes.

On the wall was a giant warning sign with a magnet and an exclamation point. On the floor, there was yellow and black tape that looked like it belonged at a crime scene. The room was oddly dim, with flickering fluorescent lights, and all the colors were shades of antiseptic beige. The atmosphere was sterile bordering on menacing.

"And the machine itself, *that I designed*, basically looked like a brick with a hole in it," Dietz said.

He knew, too, that the experience would only get worse. The girl would be fed into the claustrophobic bore of the MRI and she'd have to lie there, motionless, for 30 minutes, trying to ignore the machine's loud, alien hums and clangs.

Dietz saw the parents exchange an anguished look. They didn't know how they were going to get their daughter through the next hour.

He was crushed. In an instant, his pride had turned to horror. "It just broke my heart," said Dietz.

What he realized was that he and his designer colleagues had been focused on the *machine*: How do we make it faster? Sleeker? More powerful?

Patients, however, focused on the experience. And when they feared the MRI machine, there were real health consequences: 80% of children undergoing MRIs had to be sedated to get through the experience, and every sedation carries risks. After his epiphany in the MRI suite, Dietz reframed his mission as a designer. He wondered, what if we could design an experience that was actually *fun*?

He convened a team to help him rethink the experience: leaders of a children's museum, "design thinking" experts from Stanford, teachers at a day care center, health care staffers who worked with children, and others. The conversations helped him realize the power of a child's imagination to transform a situation.

"What is three kitchen chairs and a blanket?" he asked. To a child, it's a castle. It's a spaceship. It's a truck.

What if the MRI machine weren't an MRI machine but a spaceship? A submarine? Dietz's team reimagined the scanner as part of a larger story. One of the first rooms they designed, for the University of Pittsburgh Medical Center, was known as the Jungle Adventure. In the hallway leading into the room, the team placed stickers on the floor that looked like rocks. The kids would instinctively hop from one rock to the next. All the walls inside the room were painted in rich, colorful jungle scenes. And the rocks from the hallway led to a painted koi pond, stocked with fish, which surrounded the machine.

The MRI table lowered so that children could climb on

top. It had been redesigned to look like a hollowed-out canoe, and the kids were urged to hold still so they wouldn't tip over the canoe as it floated through the jungle. The kids readily embraced the challenge of not rocking the canoe. In his talk, Dietz mimed a kid with his arms straight down at his side with only his eyes moving. "These kids are like statues—they're frozen," he said.

Another theme was Pirate Island, where kids got to "walk the plank" to reach the machine, which was painted to look like a pirate ship. On the wall, a monkey with a pirate's bandana glided through the air on a rope swing. The supply cabinets were disguised as tiki huts.

Dietz and his colleagues stayed focused on the kids' "anxiety points," such as the loud noises made by the machines. In a San Francisco hospital, they created a Cable Car Adventure room. When kids would come in, they'd get a ticket for the car. One day, Dietz watched a hospital employee talk with a little boy: "Bobby, have you been in the cable car in the city? You remember how it was kind of noisy? So is ours!"

One day in the Pirate Island room, Dietz was talking with the mother of a girl who'd just had a scan. As they talked, the little girl kept tugging on her mom's shirt. Finally the mother said, "What is it, honey?"

The little girl asked, "Can we come back tomorrow?"

Dietz began to weep. He had transformed terror into delight.

GE's "Adventure Series," led by Dietz, have since been installed in dozens of children's hospitals, and the results have been dramatic. Children's Hospital of Pittsburgh, one of the early adopters of Dietz's design, found that the number of kids needing sedation dropped from 80% to 27%. For the shorter CT scan, only 3% of children needed sedation. The child's key moment of anxiety—lying down on a sterile table that feeds into a threatening-looking machine—has been eliminated. The kids, Dietz said, "are excited to get to the adventure, versus holding on to mom's leg. . . . Before, to get them up on the table took 10 minutes, and the scan took 4 minutes. Now they get up on the table in 1 minute, and the scan takes 4."

Because of the kids' comfort, the extra expense of the friendly designs is unimportant—since the scans go faster, the hospitals can complete more in a day.

Dietz's triumph is a story of smart, empathetic design. But it's also a story of thinking in moments. He realized that it wasn't the *machine* that needed more attention, it was the *experience*. For patients, a moment of agony was transformed into a moment of elevation. Dietz flipped a pit into a peak.

5.

Transitions should be marked, milestones commemorated, and pits filled. That's the essence of thinking in moments. To be clear, not all defining moments fit into these three categories. Many defining moments could happen anytime. The Popsicle Hotline, for instance, is a source of on-demand delight. Similarly, you could pick *any* Saturday to surprise your kids with a trip to the zoo and they probably wouldn't complain.

For most of the types of moments in this book—moments of elevation and connection and pride—almost any time is a good time. The more you can multiply them, the better. The point we're emphasizing here is that certain circumstances *demand* attention. And particularly in organizations, these circumstances tend to go unnoticed, as with the neglected first-day experience.

Here are some other examples of potential moments in organizations that cry out to be shaped:

Transitions

Promotions: Getting promoted feels good naturally, of course—it's a classic moment of pride. But it can also be a tough transition for some managers. Many people are thrust into their first managerial assignments without any training on giving feedback or motivating teams. What's needed is a managerial rite of passage that combines celebration of the honor with, say, a week's worth of shadowing and counseling by an experienced senior manager.

The first day of school: Michael J. Reimer, the principal of Roosevelt Middle School in San Francisco, wanted to help sixth graders make the transition from elementary school to junior high. He created a two-day orientation program that reviewed core math/science concepts and, more importantly, made the students comfortable navigating the school building and their more complex academic schedule. He even set up "Locker Races," which spurred students to get faster at opening their combination lockers (an unfamiliar technology for most). He said that two days later, when the seventh and eighth graders showed up, the sixth graders "felt like they owned the school."

The end of projects: In most organizations, the end of a project is commemorated by the immediate start of a new one. But it's useful to provide closure. For inspiration, consider that Steve Jobs once held a mock funeral onstage for the death of Mac Operating System 9: "Mac OS 9 was a friend to us all. He worked tirelessly on our behalf, always hosting our applications, never refusing a command, always at our beck and call, except occasionally when he forgot who he was and restarted." It was a silly but meaningful landmark in time.

Milestones

Retirement: When a person retires after a long career, the moment is a hybrid of a transition and a milestone—and for some, also a pit (due to a loss of purpose or fulfillment). Yet retirement celebrations tend toward the mundane: a sheet cake in a conference room with some hastily convened co-workers. The moment deserves so much more. In Deloitte's audit practice, retiring partners are honored at the group's annual meeting. A colleague takes the stage and tells the story of the retiree's life and career. At the end, all the partners toast the retiree, who then has a chance to address the group. It's like a winning hybrid of a wedding toast and a eulogy. (Note: We know some introverts might sooner slink into a janitor's closet than endure this, but surely there are less public ways to achieve the same thoughtfulness, for instance a keepsake book with handwritten memories from colleagues.)

Unheralded achievements: We celebrate employees' *tenure* with organizations, but what about their *accomplishments*? Isn't a salesman's 10 millionth dollar of revenue earned worth commemorating? Or what about a talented manager who has had 10 direct reports promoted?

Pits

Dealing with negative feedback: Your organization may offer 360 reviews to managers. (The 360 is a tool that collects feedback from a leader's employees, peers, and managers, thus providing a "360-degree" view of how that person is perceived.) If so, what happens if someone gets a lousy report? Are you ready with an action plan to help them escape the resulting pit?

Loss of loved ones: Employees will lose loved ones, and when they do, they deserve support. Shouldn't organizations be ready with a plan for these unpredictable moments? Imagine if a team could be assembled quickly to provide for time off, a seamless delegation of urgent tasks, and personal support (meals, child care, errands) as needed.

Life and work are full of moments that are ripe for investment. In the pages ahead, we'll learn the art of planning them.

Clinic 1
The Missed Moments of Retail Banking

Note to readers: At the end of each section, we've included a "Clinic," demonstrating how you can use the book's ideas to solve real-world problems. This Clinic focuses on the art of "thinking in moments."

The situation. Major retail banks—Citibank, Wells Fargo, PNC Bank, and others—spend billions of dollars to brand themselves as trustworthy. They also invest lavishly in technology and their physical environments to improve the "customer experience." What's shocking, though, is that even as these banks compete fiercely for customer loyalty, they seem blind to the moments that matter in those customers' lives. Customers might have a relationship with a bank that lasts for decades. Think of how many landmark moments happen in that time! And, more to the point, many of those moments *actually involve the bank:* purchasing homes, changing jobs, saving for education, weddings, retirement, etc.

The desire. Could banks learn to "think in moments"?

What moments could a retail bank create?

As we saw in this chapter, three situations constitute natural defining moments and deserve our attention: (1) transitions; (2) milestones; and (3) pits. Let's examine each category as it relates to banking relationships.

Transitions: (1) *Buying a house.* Doesn't such a big change deserve commemoration? Many realtors will leave their clients a housewarming gift. And what about the bank holding your six-figure mortgage—what kind of gift does it send? Your first monthly statement. What a missed opportunity. (2) *The first paycheck from a new job.* What if a bank sent a congratulatory note? Or a gift card for an audio book to listen to on your commute? (3) *Young person opening a first account.* At one Canadian bank, a boy brought in his piggy bank to open an account. His savings amounted to (let's say) $13.62. The teller said, "We are so proud of you for saving your money—why don't we round that up to an even $20?" The boy and his parents were thrilled, and the moment only cost a few dollars. What if bank tellers were empowered to make such gestures more frequently, making their jobs more fun and meaningful? (See the Pret A Manger story in Chapter 4 for inspiration.) (4) *Getting married.* Imagine a client calling the bank to add her spouse's name to her accounts, and then a few days later, finding that the bank had bought an item from her wedding registry! Or what if the bank offered free financial counseling to engaged couples?

Milestones: Remember how Fitbit and Pocket commemorate moments that people would otherwise have missed? (1 million words read!) Banks could easily do the same thing in countless ways, sending congratulatory messages: (1) when your savings balance reaches milestone targets such as $1,000 or $10,000; (2) when you've maintained an "emergency fund" balance for six months or one year; (3) when you've earned $100 or $1,000 in interest from the bank; (4) when you've paid off 25 or 50 or 75% of your mortgage. And then when you finally pay off your mortgage completely, wouldn't it be striking if someone from the bank personally delivered the deed to your home (now yours) and shook your hand? (Managers at one Australian bank admitted to us that not only did they *not* hand-deliver the deed, they actually *charged the clients a fee* for transferring it!)

Pits: (1) *Getting divorced or being laid off.* What if banks gave their clients the option of a three-month "pause" on their mortgage payments while they got back on their feet? The same number of mortgage payments would be made, in total, it's just that the final payment would shift three months later to accommodate the pause. This same "pause" could also be offered to new parents—"We thought you might have some new things to buy around the house, so we thought you might appreciate a few months' 'mortgage holiday'!" (2) *Assistance handling parents' affairs following death or disability.* So many people struggle in this situation—trying to untangle bills and assets and debts—and banks are in a unique position to offer counsel and support.

Final reflections: It's possible some of these suggestions are too expensive or too intrusive. (Some people might not appreciate their banks' "noticing" a new job or new spouse.) The point is that banks miss countless opportunities to boost customer loyalty by creating moments, and the lack of attention to these moments contradicts banks' talk about building strong relationships with clients. A relationship in which one party is oblivious to the most profound moments in the life of the other is no relationship at all.

Your business may not have the central role in people's lives that a bank does. But are you missing opportunities to offer support, congratulations, or counsel at critical times? Are you thinking in moments?

Moments of ELEVATION

Moments of INSIGHT

Moments of PRIDE

Moments of CONNECTION

Introduction to Moments of Elevation

So far, we've answered three key questions: *What* are defining moments? *Why* would you want to create them? And *when* should you be ready to "think in moments"? But we haven't yet addressed the most important question: *How* do we create defining moments?

As we've seen, the leaders of YES Prep created Signing Day, a defining moment for the school's graduating seniors. Doug Dietz and his colleagues created the "Adventure Series" of MRI installations, which turned a pit experience into a peak for young patients. So we know that defining moments can be consciously created. You can be the architect of moments that matter.

In the sections that follow, we'll offer some practical strategies for creating special moments using the four key elements of memorable experiences: elevation, insight, pride, and connection.

We'll begin with elevation. Moments of elevation are experiences that rise above the everyday. Times to be savored. Moments that make us feel engaged, joyful, amazed, motivated. They are peaks.

Moments of elevation can be social occasions that mark transitions: birthday parties, retirement parties, bar/bat mitzvahs, quinceañeras, and weddings.

Then there are other moments of elevation where we feel elevated by virtue of being "onstage," so to speak: competing at sporting events, giving a presentation, performing in a play. The stakes are higher. We're absorbed in the moment.

Finally, there are moments of elevation that happen spontaneously: The unplanned road trip. The walk on a sunny day that leaves you smiling. The first touch of a lover's hand.

Can we create more moments of elevation? Absolutely. We can also learn to make an existing peak "peakier"—to redesign a birthday party or client presentation to make it more memorable. The recipe for building a moment of elevation is simple, and we'll describe it in detail soon. But while elevated moments are simple to conceive, they can be maddeningly hard to bring to life. (On that subject, there's a surprising twist ahead about the John Deere "First Day Experience" story.) The absence or neglect of peaks is particularly glaring in organizations—from churches to schools to businesses—where relentless routines tend to grind them down from peaks to bumps.

In the two chapters ahead, you'll see how to find and enhance moments of elevation, and discover how hard that effort can sometimes be. You'll also see why such moments are worth fighting for. No one reflecting on their life has ever wished there had been fewer.

3

Build Peaks

1.

You are a sophomore at Hillsdale High School, a public school in San Mateo, California. In your history class, you've been studying the rise of fascism, World War II, and the Holocaust.

Meanwhile, in English, you're reading William Golding's *Lord of the Flies*, which tells the story of a group of boys who are marooned on an island. Detached from the stabilizing influences of society and culture, they revert to a state of savagery. Golding said that he wrote the novel partly as a reaction to the brutality he observed during his service in World War II. The book was his "attempt to trace the defects of society back to the defects of human nature."

One day in English, your class is discussing a part of the

novel where violence breaks out among the boys, but then the conversation is interrupted. To your surprise, you're handed an official-looking legal complaint (see below).

The document announces that William Golding has been accused of libel, for grossly misrepresenting human nature in

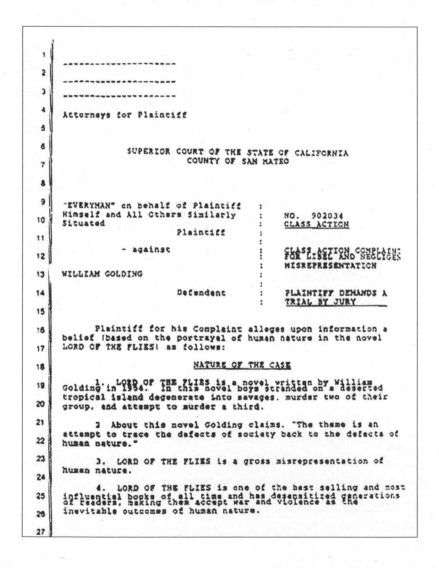

1	- -
2	- -
3	- -
4	Attorneys for Plaintiff
5	
6	SUPERIOR COURT OF THE STATE OF CALIFORNIA
7	COUNTY OF SAN MATEO
8	
9	"EVERYMAN" on behalf of Plaintiff :
10	Himself and All Others Similarly : NO. 902034
	Situated : CLASS ACTION
11	Plaintiff :
	:
12	- against : CLASS ACTION COMPLAINT
	: FOR LIBEL AND NEGLIGENT
	: MISREPRESENTATION
13	WILLIAM GOLDING :
	:
14	Defendant : PLAINTIFF DEMANDS A
	: TRIAL BY JURY
15	

        Plaintiff for his Complaint alleges upon information & belief (based on the portrayal of human nature in the novel LORD OF THE FLIES) as follows:

                        NATURE OF THE CASE

        1. LORD OF THE FLIES is a novel written by William Golding in 1954. In this novel boys stranded on a deserted tropical island degenerate into savages, murder two of their group, and attempt to murder a third.

        2 About this novel Golding claims, "The theme is an attempt to trace the defects of society back to the defects of human nature."

        3. LORD OF THE FLIES is a gross misrepresentation of human nature.

        4. LORD OF THE FLIES is one of the best selling and most influential books of all time and has desensitized generations of readers, making them accept war and violence as the inevitable outcomes of human nature.

his portrayal of the boys. You and your classmates will conduct Golding's trial. Each of you will choose a role: witness, attorney, or judge.

The trial will hinge on big, provocative questions: Was Golding right that human nature is defective? Is civilization just a veneer over a violent core?

This event takes place every year for sophomores at Hillsdale High and has become known as the Trial of Human Nature (or the Golding Trial). You and your classmates will have about two months to prepare. Then, when the day comes, you'll ride a school bus to an actual courtroom and conduct the trial in front of a jury made up of Hillsdale teachers and alumni. A gallery full of your peers and parents will watch the action.

As one of the attorneys, you will call famous witnesses from history and literature—people who have a strong opinion about the true nature of humanity, good or bad. Some predictable figures will take the stand, such as Hitler, Hobbes, Gandhi, and Mother Teresa, but the witnesses will also include some surprises: Jane Goodall, Mark Twain, Darth Vader, and even Tupac Shakur. All of them will be impersonated, in costume, by your fellow students, who will have diligently researched and rehearsed their testimonies on the question of human nature.

Over the years, many juries have convicted Golding. Many have freed him. It's up to you what will happen this time.

The Trial of Human Nature was created in 1989 by Greg Jouriles, a social studies teacher in his third year, and Susan

Bedford, an English teacher with 20 years of experience. They didn't know each other well until the time their students complained that both teachers had picked the same due date for a major assignment. That got them talking, and they realized they had a lot in common. For one thing, both had grown disillusioned with teaching and were struggling with whether they wanted to continue.

"I had fallen into the English teacher's rut of 'read a novel, talk about it, take a test,'" Bedford said. "I was looking for something that would reignite the spark that I felt at the beginning of my career."

They also craved something for their students, and as they talked, they came to a disturbing realization: Even though high school students log more time in the classroom than anywhere else, their most memorable experiences rarely take place there. Instead, they remember prom, football games, musical productions, student body elections, swim meets, talent shows.

Jouriles and Bedford then asked themselves a question that would guide the rest of their careers: *What if we could design an academic experience that was as memorable as prom?*

Think about that question. They wanted to build a peak moment. One as memorable as prom, the night when teenagers rent stretch limos and vomit on each other. That's a tall order.

They also wanted the experience to draw on some of the great themes of their courses, including a basic mystery they share: What is humanity's true nature?

Inspiration struck when Jouriles came across an account of someone conducting a mock trial of Cain, the son of Adam and Eve, who killed his brother Abel. (In the Bible, Cain is the first person who is born and also the first murderer, which is its own comment on human nature.) The mock trial format seemed perfect—it would be different, dramatic, and unpredictable.

"We purposely tried to think about ways to up the ante," said Bedford. "To give the experience more challenge, more value, to ask kids to stretch themselves in ways that virtually all of them had never stretched themselves before."

In the first year of the Trial, they raised the stakes by inviting the principal of the school and the captain of the football team, among other Hillsdale celebrities, to join the jury. They wanted their students to feel the challenge of performing in front of the school's power players.

As the weeks of preparation unfolded, Jouriles and Bedford felt some pressure of their own. If they failed, they would fail with the principal observing firsthand. "We were going through the same things the kids were going through," said Bedford. "I would never have said I'm a risk taker."*

Their confidence grew as they saw how seriously the students were taking their tasks. "There was intensity and excitement and engagement," Jouriles said, "and extra work

---

* We should note that Jouriles and Bedford were both extremely generous in sharing credit with others—both of them credited a supportive principal and school environment, and both cited a long list of intellectual influences on their work. It was our decision to keep the story focused on them for simplicity's sake.

that we never asked for. Kids were coming in after school to do more."

"The students never asked, 'How many points is this worth?'" said Bedford, incredulous. "That's *always* the first question out of kids' mouths, but they never asked it. We thought, *Whoa! We've hooked into something powerful.*"

In its first year, the Trial was far from smooth. Some witnesses were brilliant, others woefully underprepared, and others shaken by nerves. But the spectacle was unforgettable: Witnesses taking their place in a genuine Superior Court witness stand. Student attorneys, wearing suits, making oral arguments in front of an audience. Observers watching a *cross-examination of Gandhi.* It was extraordinary. When the verdict came down—not guilty!—the kids burst into cheers and applause.

After the Trial, Jouriles watched a student who had never shown much interest in the classroom "bounding down the hall like he'd just hit a game-winning shot. He said, 'That was great. What are we going to do next?'"

Since then, the Trial of Human Nature has become an institution at Hillsdale High. The fall of 2017 will see the 29th consecutive run.

Bedford and Jouriles succeeded at creating an academic event as memorable as senior prom. In fact, even more memorable. As Jouriles said, with no little pride, "In every graduation speech I've heard, the Trial has been mentioned. I've never heard prom mentioned."

The spirit of the Trial was contagious. A group of other

teachers at Hillsdale High got sick of hearing their senior class students, year after year, reminisce about how memorable the Trial was. A bit of professional jealousy kicked in. They wanted their own peak experiences for seniors. So they created the "Senior Exhibition," which challenged students to design their own research project, develop it over the course of the year, and then prepare for a final "oral defense" of their work in the spring. Topics ranged from magical realism to anorexia to the future of nuclear fusion.

Many parents attended the oral defense sessions. Their pride was obvious. "I think it's very rare for parents to see their students' work," said Jeff Gilbert, one of the creators of the Senior Exhibition and now the principal of Hillsdale High. "They see swim meets. They see dance performances. They see plays. But it's very rare for parents to see the academic work their kids do.

"School needs to be so much more like sports," he added. "In sports, there's a game, and it's in front of an audience. We run school like it is nonstop practice. You never get a game. Nobody would go out for the basketball team if you never had a game. What is the *game* for the students?"

That's thinking in moments. In essence, Gilbert is asking, "Where's the peak?" With sports, games provide peaks. We might depict a school athlete's experience in a graph like the one below—mapping a student's level of enthusiasm over the course of a week, with the three practices (all a drag) dipping below the midline and the game rising high above it, as the peak that makes the sacrifice worthwhile:

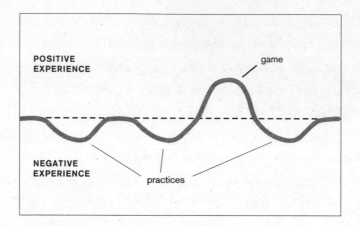

With school, though, there is a flatness to the experience. Final exams might create pits, but in general, the day-to-day emotions are pretty even:

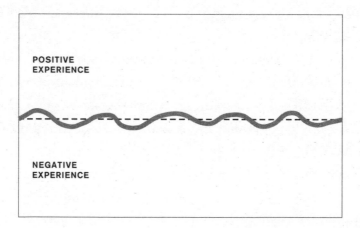

The Trial of Human Nature or the Senior Exhibition adds a peak to the flat line:

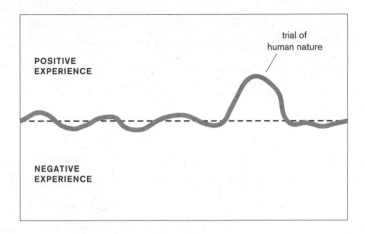

Note that this isn't costless. The time and energy invested in the Trial of Human Nature had to come from somewhere. Jouriles and Bedford sacrificed some of their free time, and it's likely they invested somewhat less time in other lessons in order to focus on the Trial.

Is this sacrifice worth it? Almost certainly yes. Recall the mantra about great service experiences from the first chapter: "Mostly forgettable and occasionally remarkable." That mantra applies to school experience (and life experience) as well. The "occasionally remarkable" moments shouldn't be left to chance! They should be planned for, invested in. They are peaks that should be built. And if we fail to do that, look at what we're left with: *mostly forgettable*.

There are more than 35,000 high schools in the United States. How many of them have even one academic experience that compares with the Trial of Human Nature? Our high schools—which were excellent public schools—certainly didn't. Did yours?

2.

While "mostly forgettable" experiences are disappointing in school and in our personal lives, they can look quite different in the business world. Here's hoping that your experiences are mostly forgettable with companies that provide you with power, water, cable, Internet, shipping, gasoline, plumbing, and dental care. That would be a success, wouldn't it? Because in many customer relationships, the moments most likely to be remembered are pits. The cable goes out. The toilet backs up. The hygienist flosses you a little too vigorously. In other words, "mostly forgettable" is actually a desirable state in many businesses! It means nothing went wrong. You got what you expected.

Think of it as the first stage of a successful customer experience. First, you fill the pits. That, in turn, frees you up to focus on the second stage: creating the moments that will make the experience "occasionally remarkable." Fill pits, then build peaks.

What's striking, though, is that many business leaders never pivot to that second stage. Instead, having filled the pits in their service, they scramble to pave the *potholes*—the minor problems and annoyances. It's as though the leaders aspire to create a complaint-free service rather than an extraordinary one.

Take the Magic Castle Hotel as an example. If the hotel lacked hot water, that would be a pit, and until it was filled, guests would not be charmed by the Popsicles. In the hotel industry, delighting your guests is an unattainable goal until you provide the basics: reasonably quick check-in, reasonably attractive rooms, reasonably comfortable beds, and so on. But some customers are still going to complain! The lamp wasn't bright enough. You didn't have HBO. There were no gluten-free Pop-Tarts on the Snack Menu.

In service businesses, there are a huge number of potholes to fix, and that's why executives can get trapped in an endless cycle of complaint management. They're always playing defense and never offense.

The Magic Castle leaders play offense. They don't try to make everything perfect. (The lobby is vaguely reminiscent of an auto service shop waiting area.) But they nail the moments that stay with you. General Manager Darren Ross is always encouraging employees to go for the moments that make a customer's jaw drop. In one case, a couple came back to the hotel one night, raving to a staffer about a cocktail they'd had at a local bar. The next day, after they returned to their room from sightseeing, they were astonished by the gift that was waiting for them. The staffer had tracked down the cocktail recipe from the bar *and bought all the ingredients so they could make their own*. That's what playing offense looks like.

(See the endnotes for one exception to this logic. Research suggests that when customers contact you because they've had problems with your product or service, you should focus on defense—that is, you should focus on efficiency and not try to "delight" them.)

"Studies have consistently shown that reliability, dependability, and competence *meet* customer expectations," said service expert Leonard Berry, a professor at Texas A&M University. "To *exceed* customer expectations and create a memorable experience, you need the behavioral and interpersonal parts of the service. You need the element of pleasant surprise.

And that comes when human beings interact." Here's the surprise, though: Most service executives are ignoring the research about meeting versus exceeding expectations.

The customer experience researchers at Forrester, a leading research and advisory firm, conduct an annual survey of more than 120,000 customers about their most recent experience with companies from a wide range of industries: banks, hotels, automakers, PC manufacturers, and more. One question in a recent survey—"The US Customer Experience Index (CX Index), 2016"—asked how the customers felt about that experience. They rated their emotions on a scale of 1 to 7, where 1 reflected a very bad feeling and 7 a very good one.

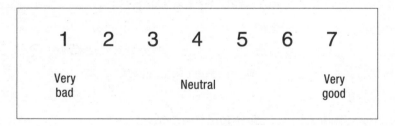

If you were a service executive, what would you do with the results of this survey question? You probably wouldn't focus on the 7s; they love you, they're happy. But given that everyone else—from the 1s to the 6s—has room for improvement, who gets the attention? Would you try to fix problems for the 1s, the people you've made miserable? Or would you try to delight the 6s to nudge them up to a 7? In an ideal world, you'd do everything at once—finding ways to vault everyone up to a 7.

In our world, though, you face trade-offs of time and attention. So which customers would you focus on?

Let's simplify the decision a bit. Say you had to choose between two plans. Plan A would magically eliminate all your unhappy customers (the 1s, 2s, and 3s), boosting them up to a 4:

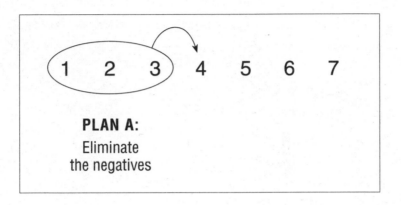

PLAN A:
Eliminate
the negatives

And Plan B would instantly vault all your neutral-to-positive customers up to a 7:

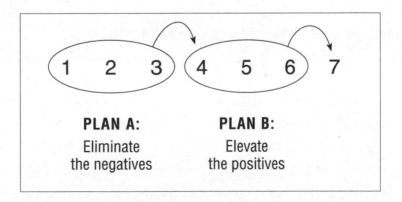

PLAN A:
Eliminate
the negatives

PLAN B:
Elevate
the positives

Which would you choose?

We've presented this scenario to dozens of executives who focus on the consumer experience, including leaders from well-regarded brands such as Porsche, Disney, Vanguard, Southwest Airlines, and Intuit, and asked them which plan better described the way their company allocated its time and resources. They estimated, on average, that their companies spent 80% of their resources trying to improve the experience of seriously unhappy customers.

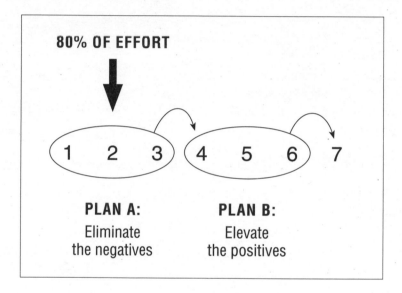

That seems reasonable at first glance—they're trying to eliminate the worst customer problems. But as a strategic investment, it's madness.

Here's why. Forrester's researchers have built models of the financial value of a customer. They know from survey responses, for instance, that an airline customer who gives a 7 (very positive) rating will spend about $2,200 on air travel over the next year. A customer giving a 4 rating, on the other hand, will spend only $800. The equivalent figures for the package shipping industry are $57 and $24.

In other words, the happiest people in any industry tend to spend more, so moving a 4 to a 7 generates more additional spending than moving a 1 to a 4. Furthermore, there are *dramatically more people* in the "feeling positive" 4–6 zone than in the "feeling negative" 1–3 zone. So, with Plan B, you're creating more financial value per person *and* reaching more people at the same time.

As a result, choosing between Plan A and Plan B is not a close call. Here's the astonishing finding from the Forrester data: If you Elevate the Positives (Plan B), you'll earn *about 9 times more revenue* than if you Eliminate the Negatives (Plan A). (8.8 times, to be precise.) Yet most executives are pursuing

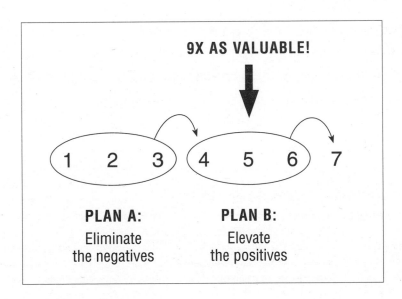

Plan A. (See the footnote for more on the methodology and an anticipated quibble.)*

How can leaders prioritize so poorly when so much money is at stake? The truth is that we should empathize with them, because we all make the same mistake in different areas of life. Research has shown, again and again, that we tend to obsess about problems and negative information. Sports fans think more about the games their teams lost than those they won. In our diaries we spend more time reflecting on the bad things that happened than the good. Negative feedback packs a heavier punch than positive; we obsess about 1 negative comment in a collection of 10 supportive ones. Researchers at the University of Pennsylvania summarized dozens of studies that pitted negative information against positive. Their conclusion was right in the title of the paper: "Bad Is Stronger than Good."

So, when it comes to the way service executives think, it's not surprising that bad is stronger than good. Their attention is naturally drawn to the customers who had the worst experiences. But in indulging that instinct, they miss an enormous opportunity.

---

* (1) Methodology: This data was drawn from an analysis of 16 industries: airlines, automotive manufacturers, auto and home insurance, retail banks, direct banks, car rental, credit cards, health insurance, hotels, PC manufacturers, parcel shipping/delivery, traditional retail, online only retail, Internet service providers, TV service providers, and wireless providers. Although there were differences across the industries, of course, the fundamental pattern we're citing was consistent. (2) The anticipated quibble. You might be thinking, "What about the negative word of mouth that might be spread by your unsatisfied customers if you don't spend your time focusing on them?" Forrester measured that effect and found that customers discouraging others from the brand was incredibly rare. The negative word-of-mouth effect was so minimal, in fact, that they eventually eliminated it from the model.

To be clear, we're not recommending that leaders abandon their efforts to fix big problems. Rather, they should reallocate their attention. There's nine times more to gain by elevating positive customers than by eliminating negative ones.

And that process of elevation—of moving customers to 7—is not about filling pits or paving potholes. To create fans, you need the remarkable, and that requires peaks. Peaks don't emerge naturally. They must be built.*

3.

How do you build peaks? You create a positive moment with elements of elevation, insight, pride, and/or connection. We'll explore those final three elements later, but for now, let's focus on elevation. To elevate a moment, do three things: First, boost sensory appeal. Second, raise the stakes. Third, break the script. (Breaking the script means to violate expectations about an experience—the next chapter is devoted to the concept.) Moments of elevation need not have all three elements but most have at least two.

Boosting sensory appeal is about "turning up the volume" on reality. Things look better or taste better or sound better or

---

* We should add that, as we got to know Forrester's team, we realized we shared a similar perspective, and we've begun to explore a consulting partnership with them that would help companies deliver better customer experiences. At press time, the partnership was not formalized, but we're intrigued by the idea of helping clients build peaks.

feel better than they usually do. Weddings have flowers and food and music and dancing. (And they need not be superexpensive—see the footnote for more.*) The Popsicle Hotline offers sweet treats delivered on silver trays by white-gloved waiters. The Trial of Human Nature is conducted in a real courtroom.

It's amazing how many times people actually wear different *clothes* to peak events: graduation robes and wedding dresses and home-team colors. At Hillsdale High, the lawyers wore suits and the witnesses came in costume. A peak means something special is happening; it should look different.

To raise the stakes is to add an element of productive pressure: a competition, a game, a performance, a deadline, a public commitment. Consider the pregame jitters at a basketball game, or the sweaty-hands thrill of taking the stage at Signing Day, or the pressure of the oral defense at Hillsdale High's Senior Exhibition. Remember how the teacher Susan Bedford said that, in designing the Trial, she and Greg Jouriles were deliberately trying to "up the ante" for their students. They made their students conduct the Trial in front of a jury that included the principal and varsity quarterback. That's pressure.

---

* Boosting sensory appeal doesn't require extravagance. Money can easily be misspent. When researchers at Emory University surveyed 3,000 people about their weddings, they found that more expensive weddings were correlated with a higher chance of divorce. That's not a statement of causation—so if you're planning a wedding, don't worry that you're endangering your marriage by splurging on flowers. But the results are a good reminder to focus on meaning rather than money. If you imagine a $1,000 wedding versus a $30,000 wedding, for instance, which one is more likely to take place in a personally meaningful, emotion-heavy location rather than a pretty but generic banquet hall? Which one is likely to feel "handmade" rather than produced?

One simple diagnostic to gauge whether you've transcended the ordinary is if people feel the need to pull out their cameras. If they take pictures, it must be a special occasion. (Not counting the selfie addict, who thinks his face is a special occasion.) Our instinct to capture a moment says: *I want to remember this.* That's a moment of elevation.

What lessens a moment are the opposite instincts: diminishing the sensory appeal or lowering the stakes. Imagine the things an unenlightened boss might say:

- Why yes, serving Popsicles to guests is a delightful idea, but honestly it's just not practical to staff a "hotline" all day, so why don't we store them in a self-serve freezer near the ice machine?
- Is it really necessary to render a verdict in the Trial of Human Nature? Shouldn't both sides come out feeling like winners?
- Yes, Signing Day is a terrific tradition, but we have so many students! What if we just printed their college choices in a program, so we can make time for an inspirational graduation speaker?

Beware the soul-sucking force of "reasonableness." Otherwise you risk deflating your peaks. Speed bumps are reasonable. Mount Everest is not reasonable.

At this point, our guess is that you like the idea of introducing more peaks in your life or work. You get it. But you may be vastly underestimating the difficulty of making it happen. The concept is simple but the execution is hard.

One reason it's hard is that it's usually no one's job to create a peak. Jouriles and Bedford were *required* to teach English and history. They were *required* to grade their students' essays and exams. But the Trial was purely optional, and to make it happen, they had to surmount countless annoying logistical and political hurdles. (Consider just one: Imagine what it would take to arrange school buses to haul students across town at a nonstandard time to a real courtroom, especially when there is no line item in the budget for such an expedition.) It would have been so easy for reasonableness to come creeping in.

As another example: Remember John Deere's First Day Experience? The program is a no-brainer, right? You may have imagined that it's been rolled out worldwide.

It hasn't. Implementation has been spotty. Lani Lorenz Fry's team, which created the experience, is part of an internal branding group. Her group *designed* the experience but it didn't control the rollout. That was left to individual John Deere offices across Asia. While in some places, such as India and Beijing, the experience has been adopted enthusiastically, in others it has been ignored altogether. Why? It's no one's job, and it's a hassle, and there's always something happening that seems more urgent.

This same dynamic is what makes it so hard to create peaks in our personal lives as well. Imagine that you and a good friend have always dreamed of seeing the northern lights. It is a "bucket list" thing for both of you. You've even pinpointed a specific place in Yukon, Canada, that would be the perfect spot to see them. What if you called that friend right now and tried to make the trip happen?

You probably have a sense of what would follow: First, three weeks of phone tag. Then initial enthusiasm ("we should totally do that!") followed by a return to normal life. Concerns about getting time off from work. Difficulty aligning calendars. What about the kids' school schedules? Money issues. Guilt about excluding partners—should they come? Sure. Okay, now there are four calendars to align and new babysitting issues.

The conclusion: "Maybe we'll try again next year?"

We're not trying to pop your balloon. Rather, we want to build your determination: It's going to be way harder than you think to create peaks. But once you've done it, you're going to consider every ounce of effort worth it. You will have created your own defining moments.

4.

Eugene O'Kelly devotes his moving memoir, *Chasing Daylight*, to making sense of an extraordinary statement that begins the book: "I was blessed. I was told I had three months to live."

In the last week of May 2005, O'Kelly's doctors told him that he suffered from the rare cancer glioblastoma multiforme. Three malignant tumors, the size of golf balls, had grown in his brain, and there was no cure. At the time, O'Kelly was 53 years old, the CEO of KPMG, the $4 billion, 20,000-employee accounting firm. He had a wife, Corinne, and two daughters. His younger daughter, Gina, 14, was still in school awaiting the summer break. Gina would likely go back to school in the fall without a father.

"All the plans that Corinne and I had made for our future had to be junked," he said. "The quicker I scrapped plans for a life that no longer existed, the better. I needed to come up with new goals. Fast." On June 8, two weeks after the diagnosis, he stepped down as the leader of KPMG. Then he did what came naturally: He made a plan. "What can I say? I was an accountant not only by trade, but manner, as well. . . . [I] did not know how to do anything unplanned—dying included."

One night at his dining room table, he drew five concentric circles. It was a map of his relationships. His family was in the center circle, and in the outer ring were more distant relationships, such as business partners. He resolved to unwind his relationships—to "beautifully resolve" them—and to work systematically from the outer circle toward the middle. He reasoned that as his disease progressed, he'd want more uninterrupted time with the people who were closest, especially his family.

He kept the first unwindings simple—a phone call or an email exchange sharing memories or mutual appreciations. He was careful not to let the conversations grow too sad or morbid; he wanted them to be special.

The third and fourth circles were composed of closer friends and colleagues, and he met with them in person. O'Kelly wanted their encounters to be full of "pleasure and pleasures." Sometimes they shared an exquisite meal. Other times, they met in a beautiful place: sitting at a park bench by the water or strolling through Central Park (boosting sensory appeal in an atmosphere of heightened stakes). In these unwindings, O'Kelly and his friends swapped stories and talked about life. He expressed gratitude for their friendship.

He came to think of these peaks as Perfect Moments, and his mission, as he saw it, was to create as many of them as he could in his dwindling time.

As the summer went on, he began to spend more time with his closest friends and family. He had moved to the center circle. He said goodbye to his sisters, Rose and Linda, and then, in August, he and Corinne and Gina went to stay at their second home, in Lake Tahoe, Nevada. By then O'Kelly had endured a regimen of radiation intended to shrink his tumors and earn him a few more weeks of life. He was very weak.

In late August, his mother and brother flew to Tahoe for the weekend. It would be their final unwinding visit. On Sunday, which was a beautiful day, they took a boat out onto the lake.

O'Kelly wrote, "After we were out there a while, I took my mother's hand and walked her to the front of the boat to talk, just the two of us. I told her I was in a good place. I told her I would see her in heaven. A person of deep faith, she was comfortable with that. . . . It was a perfect day. I felt complete. Spent but complete."

The evening after his mother and brother left, Corinne lay in his arms on the couch. She sensed that he was starting to go and commented on his "absence." He said, "You're going to have to take over now. I've done all I can do."

About two weeks later, on September 10, 2005, O'Kelly died of a pulmonary embolism.

What O'Kelly realized, in the shadow of his final days, was the extraordinary power of a moment. He wrote:

I experienced more Perfect Moments and Perfect Days in two weeks than I had in the last five years, or than I probably would have in the next five years, had my life continued the way it was going before my diagnosis. Look at your own calendar. Do you see Perfect Days ahead? Or could they be hidden and you have to find a way to unlock them? If I told you to aim to create 30 Perfect Days, could you? How long would it take? Thirty days? Six months? Ten years? Never? I felt like I was living a week in a day, a month in a week, a year in a month.

Now, take a second look at the beginning of O'Kelly's memoir, especially those final two words: "I was blessed. I was told I had three months *to live*."

That opportunity *to live* was why he felt blessed. Shouldn't we share his zeal for moments that matter? We may have more time to live than he did, but should that be a reason to put them off?

This is the great trap of life: One day rolls into the next, and a year goes by, and we still haven't had that conversation we always meant to have. Still haven't created that peak moment for our students. Still haven't seen the northern lights. We walk a flatland that could have been a mountain range.

It's not easy to snap out of this tendency. It took a terminal illness for Gene O'Kelly to do it.

What would it take to motivate you to create a Perfect Moment?

4

Break the Script

1.

Chris Hurn's son would not go to sleep. It was the boy's first night home from a vacation in Amelia Island, Florida, and he had accidentally left behind Joshie, his beloved stuffed giraffe. There was no sleeping without Joshie. Yet Joshie was in Florida. So Hurn was left with a predicament.

In the long tradition of parents desperate to get their kids to sleep, Hurn assessed his options and concluded that he'd better start lying. "Joshie is fine," he told his son. "He's just taking an extra-long vacation at the resort." His son seemed to buy it, eventually drifting off to sleep.

Later that night, to Hurn's great relief, a Ritz-Carlton staffer called to report that Joshie had been found. Hurn asked the staffer a favor. He explained what he'd told his son and asked if someone at the Ritz could take a picture of Joshie on a lounge chair by the pool, to show he'd been vacationing.

A few days later, Joshie arrived—along with a binder full of pictures. One showed Joshie lounging by the pool, another showed Joshie driving a golf cart. Others captured him hanging with the hotel parrot, getting a massage in the spa (with cucumber slices covering his eyes), and even monitoring the security cameras in the control room.

Hurn and his wife were delighted, and their son was ecstatic. Hurn wrote a blog post about the experience, which went viral.

Why did everyone love the story of Joshie? Because it shattered our expectations. What do we expect to happen when a boy loses a stuffed animal on vacation? For it to be returned, maybe. If he's lucky. (And if so, it would probably be crumpled inside a box to reduce postage.)

Instead, someone at the Ritz spent a few hours zipping around the resort with a stuffed giraffe, snapping absurd pics— "somebody get some cucumber slices for his eyes!"—so they could please some guests *who had already checked out and gone home*. It was a strange and magical thing to do.

The staff at the Ritz broke the script. The term *script*, used this way, dates back to some research from the 1970s; it refers to our expectations of a stereotypical experience. As an example, the "restaurant script" runs something like this: We walk in the door. Someone greets us, shows us to a table, and hands us menus. Then someone else brings over glasses of water. Our waiter stops by to take drink orders. And so on. That's the way restaurants work.

The psychologists Roger Schank and Robert Abelson used the concept of a script to explain how our brains store and access knowledge. For instance, consider this simple scenario:

JOHN ORDERED A HAMBURGER.
IT CAME OUT COLD.
HE LEFT A SMALL TIP.

The scenario is easy to visualize, which is odd, because it never mentions a waiter or a plate or a table or even a restaurant. Our underlying restaurant script supplies all the missing details. Now consider a different scenario:

HARRIET WENT TO JACK'S BIRTHDAY PARTY.
THE CAKE TASTED AWFUL.
HARRIET LEFT JACK'S MOTHER A VERY SMALL TIP.

Wait, what? We have a clear "birthday party script": parents giving gifts, friends eating cake, kids learning to bludgeon animals until candy comes out. But we never tip Jack's mother—ever. The story breaks a script.

In the last chapter, we saw that creating moments of elevation involves boosting sensory pleasures and raising the stakes. Breaking the script—defying people's expectations of how an experience will unfold—is the third method.

Isn't "breaking the script" just surprise by a different name? Yes, surprise is what makes the moment memorable. But the takeaway isn't quite as simple as "Surprise people!" Surprise is cheap and easy. If your local power company promoted "Blackout Tuesdays!" that would be surprising (especially if that event was meant to store up energy for "Bug Zapper Saturdays!"). But that surprise accomplishes nothing.

Breaking the script isn't just surprise, it's strategic surprise. The Ritz-Carlton created the Joshie photo album because it wants to be known for its extraordinary service. It wasn't simply a random act of kindness.

The other difference between "breaking the script" and generic surprise is that the former forces us to think about the *script*. Our lives are filled with scripts: The script for how your family spends Sundays. The script for your team's staff meetings. The script for a hotel check-in. To break the script, we've first got to understand the script.

The script of eating at McDonald's is so familiar that it's a source of comfort. It's nice to know that, anywhere in the world, you'll understand exactly what to expect. But here's the problem: Familiarity and memorability are often at odds. Who cherishes the memory of the last time they ate at McDonald's? If you're looking to create memorable moments for your customers, you've got to break the script.

A study of hotel reviews on TripAdvisor found that, when guests reported experiencing a "delightful surprise," an astonishing 94% of them expressed an unconditional willingness to recommend the hotel, compared with only 60% of guests who were "very satisfied." And "very satisfied" is a high bar! Surprise matters. (Think of the Popsicle Hotline.) But how can you possibly replicate "delightful surprises"?

In some ways, the Magic Castle Hotel has it easy, because its guests might only stay there once or twice in a lifetime. The

Popsicle Hotline never gets old. What if your customers come weekly or even daily? That's trickier.

Imagine, for instance, that a coffee shop owner decided to give away free biscotti every Friday. On the first Friday of the giveaway, it would be a delightful surprise. But by the fourth Friday, the free biscotti would be an *expectation*. If the offer were ever discontinued, it's easy to imagine customers (ungrateful wretches!) actually complaining about it.

So how do you break the script consistently enough that it matters—but not so consistently that customers adapt to it? One solution is to introduce a bit of randomness. At the café chain Pret A Manger, for example, regular customers noticed that, every now and then, they'd be given something for free with their order. One service expert wrote, of getting free coffee, "It has happened a few times over the last few years, too often for it to be a coincidence, yet so infrequent that it is unexpected. This makes me feel valued as a customer, puts a smile on my face and encourages me to visit again."

These "spontaneous" gifts are only half-spontaneous, as it turns out. Pret A Manger employees are allowed to give away a certain number of hot drinks and food items every week. Pret CEO Clive Schlee said of his staffers, "They will decide 'I like the person on the bicycle' or 'I like the guy in the tie' or 'I fancy that girl or that boy.' It means 28% of people have had something free."

Think on that. Almost a third of customers have gotten something free at least once. (Probably more than once, if they have dimples.)

Other retail chains provide discounts or freebies to customers who use loyalty cards, of course, but Schlee told the *Standard* newspaper he rejected that approach: "We looked at loyalty cards but we didn't want to spend all that money building up some complicated Clubcard-style analysis."

This is ingenious. Pret A Manger has restored the surprise and humanity to perks that, in a loyalty card scheme, would have been systematized. Note that the giveaways are satisfying for the staff as well as the customers. In an industry where rules tend to govern every employee behavior, it's a relief for employees to be given some discretion: *Hey, every week, give away some stuff to whomever you like.* It broke the script for them, too. In the service business, a good surprise is one that delights employees as well as customers.

Another example of good surprise comes from Southwest Airlines, which has thrived by offering passengers the combination of low fares and friendly service. Southwest's flight attendants try to have fun with even the boring parts of the job, like making the flight safety announcements. Many of their cheeky safety announcements have gone viral over the years; in fact, there's a "wall of fame" at Southwest headquarters that commemorates some of the best jokes:

- Ladies and gentlemen, if you wish to smoke, the smoking section on this airplane is on the wing and if you can light 'em, you can smoke 'em.
- To activate the flow of oxygen, pull down on the mask, place it over your nose and mouth, then insert one quarter for the first five minutes of oxygen and an additional dime every five minutes after. Exact change only, please!

- If you should get to use the life vest in a real-life situation, the vest is yours to keep.
- Put the oxygen mask on yourself first, then on your child. If you're traveling with more than one child, start with the one who has more potential or who is less likely to put you in the home.

These wisecracks create peaks—they break the script of the usual monotonous announcements. But what are they *worth*? Do they have any economic value? In a workshop with the Southwest analytics team—the people who analyze customer data looking for helpful insights—Chip asked them, "How many extra flights does a customer take when they hear a funny flight safety announcement?"

There was silence in the room. They had never asked that question before. But they also knew that they *could* answer it—they had the right data. Southwest, like many companies, has obsessive amounts of customer data. Unlike most companies, though, they had the data in a form that could be used to make critical decisions. The analytics team had previously figured out, for instance, that passengers are forgiving of short flight delays, but past 25 or 30 minutes, they become less likely to take future flights with Southwest. As a result, Southwest's executives evaluated purchasing two additional Boeing 737s as reserve aircraft, providing a backup option when other planes had to be taken out of service. The investment would not eliminate delays but it would mitigate them. Total cost? Roughly $50–70 million per plane, for a total of around $120 million.

Intrigued by the safety announcement question, the insights team, including Frank Tooley, Katie Boynton, and Michael

Overly, dug into the customer data. In the company's surveys, about 1 in every 70 customers will mention, unprompted, that they heard a funny flight safety announcement. The insights team used those surveys to identify all the passengers on that same flight, since they all would have heard the same announcement.

The team was particularly interested to analyze the habits of customers who travel more than once per year on Southwest; let's call them "loyal customers." (Other passengers fly so infrequently, it's hard to detect changes in their behavior.) Here's what the analysis showed: When loyal customers were on a flight with a funny flight safety announcement, they flew one half-flight more over the next year than did similar customers who hadn't heard one. (These are averages, of course, since it's difficult to fly a half-flight without a parachute.)

What's the value of those extra half-flights? The analytics group calculated that if Southwest could double the number of customers hearing a funny flight safety announcement, the result would be more than $140 million in revenue! That's more than the cost of two 737s. But the revenue figure is an *annual* number—in other words, every single year that you could maintain the comedic performance, you'd earn extra revenue equal to the price tags of two jets. Just because your crew told some more jokes. That's an astonishing return on investment, given that there is no real financial investment at all. (You don't even need to train the attendants, really—just circulate recordings or transcripts of the funny bits.) As we saw with Pret A Manger, there's great value in good surprise.

The serial entrepreneur Scott Beck believes that good surprise is a fundamental principle of retail businesses. Beck, who had top leadership positions in three enormous retail chains—Blockbuster Video, Boston Chicken, and Einstein Bros—said that the secret to growing a business is to "reduce negative variance and increase positive variance." To reduce negative variance is to prevent stores from operating differently in a way that harms the customer experience. If one Einstein Bros store toasts a bagel perfectly and another burns it half the time, that's negative variance. To manage the problem, store owners need systems that ensure the bagels are toasted right every time.

But Beck believes it's a mistake to squeeze the "variance" out of the way customers are treated. Certainly there should be a baseline level of service: Employees should be polite and make eye contact. What customers want and need, though, will vary a great deal. Some customers want small talk, others want speed. Some are in a bubbly mood, others have dried tears under their eyes. To increase positive variance is to welcome humanity and spontaneity into the system. And that means giving employees license to break the script.

This insight applies not just to employees, but also to parents. In families, so often we are hustling to "minimize negative variance"—getting kids to school on time, managing household chaos, keeping sibling spats under control. But are we focusing as much energy on increasing positive variance from week to week?

As an example, in researching this book, we periodically tried out exercises with groups of people to see whether they were finding the book's ideas practical. One of our most popular exercises was what we called "Saturday Surprise." The instructions were incredibly simple: Break the script on your Saturday routines.

People seemed to have a blast doing this. Two broke roommates pooled their gas money to check out Red Rocks, a famous amphitheater in Colorado surrounded by rock outcroppings. A romantic husband prepared a Saturday evening picnic for his wife on the San Antonio Riverwalk. A woman asked her daughter to plan the day's activities and was astonished when she (the daughter) came back with an hour-by-hour logistical plan. (The woman said, "I'm an engineer, so my heart just sang!")

The Saturday Surprise yielded bite-sized defining moments. Just by disrupting routines, we can create more peaks.

2.

Peaks spice up our experience. They can enrich high school education (the Trial) and garnish flights (Southwest) and delight children (Joshie's vacation). In that sense, they are evergreen — they can happen at any time and retain their power of elevation. But don't forget that peaks can also be used to mark transitions. (Think weddings and graduations.) Executives who are leading change should be deliberate about creating peaks that demarcate the shift from the "old way" to the "new way." The heart of change, after all, is the need to break the script.

In 2008, the CEO of VF Corporation asked Stephen Dull, the vice president of strategy, to head up an effort to make the company more innovative. Dull and a colleague he had recently hired, Soon Yu, led the innovation project, and the two of them prepared an insightful, data-rich presentation describing their plan. The duo, both former consultants, kept adding clever refinements to the plan, until their final PowerPoint presentation weighed in at 120 slides.

Then, two months before they were due to present the plan company-wide, Dull lost faith in the approach and scrapped it. He realized that if they were going to succeed, they had to break the script.

The situation at VF was complicated. You may not recognize the company's name, but it owns a portfolio of famous fashion brands, including Wrangler and Lee Jeans, Vans, Nautica, JanSport, Timberland, and The North Face. Traditionally, the brands had been run autonomously, with the holding company VF Corporation staying in the background providing financial and logistical support. But when the economy crashed in 2008, the company hit a wall, and the top executives began to reconsider the strategy of running VF like a loose confederacy.

The brands North Face and JanSport, for instance, had a lot in common: Both were outdoors focused, and they even marketed similar products, such as backpacks. In San Leandro, California, the teams shared a facility, separated by a wall that was cubicle-height. Yet, according to Yu, "that wall was treated as the equivalent of the Korean DMZ. They would not talk to each other. They would not share information with each other, yet they were talking to the same vendors, creating pretty much the same thing. But they weren't sharing any ideas."

The brands were not just independent, they were insular. They'd become too dependent on the whims of their "merchants," who are the people in fashion businesses responsible for anticipating consumer tastes. "There's a temptation to say, 'Well, consumers don't know what they want three years from now,'" said Yu, "'so I'm going to *tell them* what they want.'"

Putting so much trust in the merchants dulled the brands' instinct to *learn*. They stopped getting closer to the customer, stopped obsessing about competitors, and stopped looking for new partnerships. And that, in essence, was the cultural stagnation that Dull and Yu were trying to reverse. They wanted the brands to learn from each other and, more than that, to learn from the giant world outside their doors.

When Dull decided to scrap the 120 PowerPoint slides, he and Yu had to restart from scratch. What they realized was that they didn't need their colleagues to *understand* something, they needed them to *feel* something. And it had to happen at the leadership meeting scheduled for September 2010 in Los Angeles.

"We decided we had to change absolutely everything about the meeting that was to take place," said Dull. "What's the standard? Well, you go to a place and you have the same universal metal chair that's uncomfortable, around round tables, in some low-ceiling conference room. And you have speaker after mind-numbing speaker, mostly internal . . . and that's your leadership meeting."

Dull devised a plan to break the script at that meeting. Culture change is difficult and slow. To have any chance to succeed, the meeting needed to deliver a jolt.

When their 150 colleagues arrived in the ballroom in Los Angeles, there were no tables and chairs. Just sofas, with enough room for all of them. VF Corporation CEO Eric Wiseman stood up to kick off the meeting. "Everyone sort of prepared to nestle in for a 30-minute opening," said Dull. But instead something else happened. Wiseman announced that the group would spend its two-day meeting "going outside for new ideas."

Within five minutes, everyone was walking outside to board buses headed to a variety of different locations. One group participated in a beauty science workshop, where professionals did the makeup for each person in the group, helped them select an outfit, and then posed them for a photo shoot. Another group "tagged" a building (legally) with graffiti artists in inner-city L.A. Other groups took surfing lessons in Malibu, practiced improv comedy, or cooked a meal with Wolfgang Puck.

"Most organizations have people *think* about a PowerPoint pitch with the hope that they will *feel* something and then *do* something different," said Yu. "Let's face it: Most PowerPoints aren't creating a lot of emotion. We decided to flip this on its head. Let's have people *do* something active and immersive. That's going to generate more of an emotional response so they will *feel* something. And then they can *think* about what they've learned."

At the two-day leadership conference, Dull and Yu accomplished something vital: In essence, they had dramatized the company's new strategy. *Being innovative starts with getting outside the office, and it doesn't "hurt," it feels good! It stimulates you and stretches you and reinvigorates you.*

The retreat generated enthusiasm for the new approach to innovation, and when their colleagues returned home, they started embracing the "go outside" message. At JanSport, a leading maker of backpacks, "We had always thought of ourselves as the 'carry stuff' brand, for people who were carrying things from Point A to Point B," said President Steve Munn. But as they began to observe the way people were using their bags—from commuters and students to more "extreme" users such as mountain climbers and homeless people—they realized that people weren't just *carrying* the bags, they were unpacking them and using them in "third spaces" like coffee shops or buses or libraries. What if the backpack of the future could serve as a kind of portable desk, with built-in outlets for your devices and a master extension cord ready to be jacked into the wall at Starbucks?

A group at Wrangler met with some structural engineers, and the conversation turned to cantilevers, or structures that are anchored on only one side. Think of a diving board or a balcony, where one side is secured so well that the other part can hang off, seemingly unsupported. Many bridges and buildings are built with similar features.

Cantilevered designs allow unwieldy structures to be supported and elevated with elegance. *Aha!* thought the Wrangler team, *we'd like to do that with buttocks!* And thus was born Wrangler Booty Up jeans. Later, another VF brand called Lucy incorporated the same insight—a great example of the "mutual learning" that Dull and Yu had desired among the company's brands.

In the six years after the launch in Los Angeles, VF has

grown its revenue from $7 billion to $13 billion, with most of that increase fueled by organic growth rather than acquisition. VF now has a pipeline of innovative products, estimated in value at $1.6 billion by Dull, that are in the process of design and testing en route to retail shelves. These products were created and nurtured by a corporate culture that has learned the value of going outside for ideas and inspiration.

And the defining moment of that cultural evolution was the leadership meeting in Los Angeles. From the sofas to the buses to the creative expeditions, the meeting was designed to deliver strategic surprise.

3.

For business leaders, breaking the script is a strategy—a way of creating moments that support the company's brand or, as with VF, reinforce a change in strategy. But beyond the world of organizations, breaking the script has a broader significance. The principle helps to explain why we remember what we do, and it sheds light on one of the most interesting mysteries of memory, which is called the "reminiscence bump."

In a study by Dorthe Berntsen and David Rubin, respondents were prompted to think about the life of a baby who had just been born and to predict what would be "the most important events that are likely to take place in this infant's life." The ten most commonly cited events were as follows (shown in order). See if you notice any patterns:

1. Having children
2. Marriage
3. Begin school
4. College
5. Fall in love
6. Others' death
7. Retirement
8. Leave home
9. Parents' death
10. First job

It's striking that 6 out of the 10 most important events all happen during a relatively narrow window of time: roughly age 15 to 30. (This 6 out of 10 calculation presumes that marriage and kids happen within that window, which of course isn't true of everyone but is true for most people.)

Similarly, if you ask older people about their most vivid memories, research shows, they tend to be drawn disproportionately from this same period, roughly ages 15 to 30. Psychologists call this phenomenon the "reminiscence bump." Why does a 15-year period in our lives—which is not even 20% of a typical life span—dominate our memories?

"The key to the reminiscence bump is novelty," said Claudia Hammond in her book *Time Warped*. "The reason we remember our youth so well is that it is a . . . time for firsts—first sexual relationships, first jobs, first travel without parents, first experience of living away from home, the first time we get much real choice over the way we spend our days."

Novelty even changes our perception of time. In an experiment conducted by Vani Pariyadath and David Eagleman of Baylor College of Medicine, participants were shown a series of images. Most of them were identical, but every now and then, a new image would appear: brown shoe, brown shoe, brown shoe, brown shoe, alarm clock, brown shoe, brown shoe, and so on. Even though all the images were displayed for the same amount of time, it didn't feel that way to the participants. They were convinced that the alarm clock—the pattern-breaking image—was displayed longer. This misperception has become known as the "oddball effect."

Eagleman, a neuroscientist, argued that what causes the oddball effect is, in effect, your brain's boredom with the brown-shoe picture. The first time you see it, you examine the picture carefully. Your memory is "taking notes" rapidly. But with each repetition of the image, you devote less and less energy to inspecting it. By the seventh time, a quick glance tells you that, well, it's just that same shoe again. Then, when you see the anomalous alarm clock, you start logging notes again. The resulting gap in the "density" of your memory—copious notes for the alarm clock, sparse notes for the repetitive shoe—leads to the misperception that the alarm clock picture was displayed longer.

In other words, surprise stretches time. In supporting this insight, Eagleman has embraced some rather extreme research methods. He is famous for an experiment in which he asks volunteers to leap off a 150-foot platform and free-fall into a net. Afterward, they are asked to estimate how long the fall took, and their estimates are, on average, too high by 36%. Their fear and focus make time seem to expand. (So here's one tip to live a "longer" life: Scare the hell out of yourself, regularly.)

This is the intuitive explanation for the common perception that time seems to accelerate as we get older. Our lives become more routine and less novel. We're seeing more and more brown shoes and fewer alarm clocks.

Now, that's a somewhat depressing realization. Have we really left our most memorable days behind us?

Yes, probably. And that's also probably a good thing. Because it would be very easy to create a second reminiscence bump late in life. Just divorce your spouse, quit your job, move to New Zealand, and become a shepherd. Plenty of novelty there, and you're certain to write a rush of memories. But let's not confuse memorability with wisdom.

For those anxious about facing a future that's less memorable than the past, our advice is to honor the old saw, "Variety is the spice of life." But notice that it does not say, "Variety is the entrée of life." Nobody dines on pepper and oregano. A little novelty can go a long way. Learn to recognize your own scripts. Play with them, poke at them, disrupt them. Not all the time—just enough to keep those brown shoes looking fresh.

By breaking the script, we can lay down a richer set of memories. As the authors of the book *Surprise* put it, "We feel most comfortable when things are certain, but we feel most alive when they're not."

MOMENTS OF ELEVATION
THE WHIRLWIND REVIEW

1. Moments of elevation are experiences that rise above the routine. They make us feel engaged, joyful, amazed, motivated.
   - *Examples: Birthday parties, weddings, football games, public speeches, or spontaneous road trips.*

2. Some activities have built-in peaks, such as games or recitals or celebrations. But other areas of life can fall depressingly flat.
   - *High school principal: "We run school like it is nonstop practice. You never get a game."*

3. Here's our three-part recipe to *create* more moments of elevation: (1) Boost the sensory appeal; (2) Raise the stakes; (3) Break the script. Usually elevated moments have 2 or 3 of those traits.
   - *The Trial of Human Nature has all three parts: (1) Sensory appeal: The costumes, the real courtroom. (2) Raised stakes: One side will win and capture the glory. (3) Break the script: Everything about the Trial defies the normal rhythms of school.*

4. The third part—break the script—requires special attention. To break the script is to defy people's expectations of how an experience will unfold. It's strategic surprise.
   - *The Ritz staffers broke the script with their playful photo album for a boy's lost "Joshie" toy.*

5. Moments that break the script are critical for organizational change. They provide a demarcation point between the "old way" and the "new way."
   - *VF Corporation ended its leadership meeting after a few minutes*

and challenged people to "go outside," participating in surfing classes or improv comedy.

6. The most memorable periods of our lives are times when we break the script.
   - *Recall the "reminiscence bump," a period full of novelty: our first kiss, our first job, etc.*
   - *Novelty actually seems to slow down time. That's why we feel like time goes faster as we age.*

7. Caution: Even with the simple three-part recipe, moments of elevation can be hard to build. They are no one's "job" and they are easy to delay or water down.
   - *Beware the soul-sucking force of reasonableness: "Couldn't we just put the Popsicles in a cooler by the ice machine?"*

8. But building peaks is worth the struggle. They provide some of the most memorable moments of our lives.
   - *Eugene O'Kelly, in his dying days, found fulfillment in his "Perfect Moments."*

--------------------   **Clinic 2**   --------------------
How Do You Refresh a Meeting That's Grown Rote?

Note to readers: This Clinic and the three others that follow later are designed to model how you can use the book's core framework (Elevation, Insight, Pride, and Connection) to create defining moments. They are not specific to the chapters you've just read; we want them to cut across the sections and remind you to keep thinking about the full framework.

The situation: Rev. Matthew Frey is the rector of the Episcopal Church of the Redeemer in Eagle Pass, Texas, a town about a mile from a border crossing with Mexico. Every month he meets with the vestry, the church's board of elders. It's the kind of meeting that will be familiar to many nonprofits and religious organizations: As Frey said, "We review the old business, then the new business, then the treasurer's report, and then we talk about how much money we do *not* have. We fall into the same patterns."

The desire: Frey wanted to breathe new life into the meeting. How could he make the meeting exciting—the source of new ideas—rather than feeling like an administrative obligation? He was particularly keen to get the vestry thinking about ways to improve the experience of first-time visitors to the church.

How Do We Create a Defining Moment?

What's the moment? (1) In this case, there's no mystery—Frey should choose to do something special at one of the scheduled vestry meetings. (2) Of course, Frey should also be alert to other key transition points in the life of the vestry, for instance when new elders join and others rotate off. (3) For the sake of this Clinic, we will focus on the meeting. Note that we will introduce principles below that we will discuss in greater detail later in the book; some of the terminology may be unfamiliar but you'll get the gist.

Add ELEVATION:

1: Break the script. That's what Frey did. When the vestry showed up for the meeting, he greeted them with pads of paper and pens and sorted them into groups of two or three. He gave them a challenge: Imagine that you are visiting this church for the first time. Roam the grounds for 15 or 20 minutes. What do you notice? The elders came back with a range of observations:

    a. We have bilingual services but all our signage is in English!

    b. There was an Alcoholics Anonymous meeting going on in our building—we had no idea so many people attended it. Are there other ways we can open our facilities to the public? And how can we make sure they know they're invited to worship with us?

    c. I'd forgotten how beautiful this church is!

2: Raise the stakes. Frey could have gone further. What if he had challenged the vestry, based on their observations, to make recommendations to the congregation about improving the visitor experience? That might have added some pressure/accountability.

3: Boost sensory appeal. Frey's challenge to walk the grounds already added a sense of play to the moment. What if he had also given them a "character" to role-play during their observations? For example, "You are a 28-year-old Hispanic single mother with two children, and you've just moved here. You're anxious about school choices and a friend told you about our day school. You wonder if it's right for your kids." That might have made it even easier to see the church with fresh eyes.

Add INSIGHT:

1: Trip over the truth. Frey's activity allowed the vestry to *discover* insights for themselves. The resulting ideas (adding signage in Spanish, inviting other community groups to use the church's facilities) became *their ideas* as a result. They might have been more resistant, or less excited, had those same ideas emerged from a congregational "suggestion box."

2: Stretch for insight. Frey might use a future vestry meeting to challenge the elders to *become* visitors themselves, perhaps by attending another church or a community meeting. What does it feel like to be the new person in the group? Which groups do a good job of integrating you quickly, and what can we learn from them?

Add PRIDE:

1: Multiply milestones. The vestry could celebrate certain moments of accomplishment—say, the first time a new member joins after having discovered the church at a community meeting hosted on its grounds.

2: Recognize others. The elders could recognize and praise parishioners who go out of their way to be hospitable to visitors.

Add CONNECTION:

1: Role-playing, as suggested above, is a way to create an empathic connection between the vestry and parishioners whose life situations might be very different.

2: Create shared meaning. Frey could build connections *among the vestry*. For instance, Frey could have started a meeting by asking the vestry to reflect on times when the church had been at its best—and at its worst—in accommodating visitors. Those kinds of shared personal reflections can reconnect people with the meaning of their work.

Final reflections: Frey said that the "roaming the grounds" exercise had a powerful effect: "People are still talking about the things they saw that day." If you have a standing meeting in your organization, you've got a great opportunity to create a moment that refreshes and rejuvenates the participants. Not every meeting needs to be a "defining moment." But once every 5 to 10 meetings, find a way to break the script.

Moments of ELEVATION

Moments of INSIGHT

Moments of PRIDE

Moments of CONNECTION

Introduction to Moments of Insight

What if a defining moment in someone's life is not a moment of elevation? What if, instead, it's an awful moment?

Asked about a defining moment in his career, one man wrote: "In my first job I was rated at the bottom of my starting class and did not get the 'parity' raise that all my peers got—which meant I was making less than the incoming class of hires. It was the first time I really failed at something and it was a wake-up call that the skills I had mastered in school were not the skills that would help me in the work world."

Now, that sounds nothing like a moment of elevation! He's not feeling joyful or engaged or "above the ordinary." He's been blindsided by negative feedback. Yet it's not just an emotional low point, either. It's a low point that holds the promise of a *better* future path. *Ouch—I need to change things to make sure that doesn't happen again.*

Moments of insight deliver realizations and transformations. Some insights are small but meaningful. At your favorite coffee shop, you sample coffees from South America and Africa and you notice how different the flavors are. That adds insight to a transactional experience. At a rehearsal dinner, you tell a funny story about the groom that also reveals something about his character. That adds insight to a social experience.

What we'll explore ahead are the larger moments of insight, the ones that deliver a jolt. Sometimes the emotions are dark: *I'm no good at this.* Or, *I don't believe in what I'm doing anymore.* Other moments of insight can also be wildly positive: *This is the person I'm going to spend the rest of my life with!* Or the "eureka!" moment of creative discovery.

Many moments of insight are serendipitous. Lightning strikes, and there's no explaining why. You can't schedule epiphanies.

But these experiences are not wholly out of our control. We'll explore two strategies for *creating* moments of insight. We can cause others to "trip over the truth" (Chapter 5). And when we need to understand ourselves better, we can "stretch for insight" (Chapter 6).

In the pages ahead are stories of sharp emotion—disgust, enlightenment, heartbreak, and exhilaration. But we begin with the story of a shocking realization you won't soon forget.

5

Trip Over the Truth

1.

In 2007, the *British Medical Journal* asked its readers to vote on the most important medical milestone that had occurred since 1840, when the *BMJ* was first published. Third place went to anesthesia, second place to antibiotics. The winner was one you might not have expected: the "sanitary revolution," encompassing sewage disposal and methods for securing clean water.

Much of the world, though, is still waiting for that revolution to come.

In 2016, there were about a billion people worldwide who lacked access to clean water, and also a billion (likely many of the same people) who, lacking toilets, defecated outdoors—often in areas used by multiple people. This practice of open defecation has dire health consequences, just as it did in 1840.

It leads to the mass spread of diseases, among them cholera, hookworm, roundworm, and schistosomiasis, that cause people to suffer or die.

How could you end the practice of open defecation? The answer may seem obvious: provide latrines. And for years, that was the strategy of many development organizations. In a typical example, WaterAid funded the construction of latrines in 1999 in some villages in northern Bangladesh. To ensure that the project had been executed successfully, they invited an outside expert named Dr. Kamal Kar to conduct an evaluation of the work. He traveled to the site in Bangladesh, and that's where our story begins.

Warning to readers: The story ahead is full of disgusting images, and it also makes frequent use of the "s-word" for feces. We do not use this term gratuitously; indeed, it's the very heart of the story. But if you prefer to avoid the word, we recommend that you skip ahead to the next section, labeled "2."

In Bangladesh, Kar found that the project had gone exactly as planned. The latrines were well built and many people used them. But he also found something else: "I would walk behind the villages and go into the fields, and in every village we went in, I stepped on shit," he said. Open defecation was still rampant. And he knew that, as soon as rainy season came, the shit would disperse all around the village.*

---

* Kar believes that it's a mistake to soft-pedal the word using medical terms such as *feces*, or more kid-friendly terms such as *poop* or *doodoo*. When he works in new countries, he makes sure to ask for the crude slang term for shit. He wants the word to shock.

It wasn't enough, in other words, for *some* people to use the latrines or even half. To solve the village's health problems, it had to become the norm.

It was an eye-opening moment for him. The world's development organizations had been thinking about open defecation as a hardware problem: If we just distribute enough latrines, we will solve the problem. But it wasn't that simple. For some villagers, the latrines seemed like a solution to a problem that they hadn't asked to be solved. Sometimes the latrines would be disassembled, with their parts used for other purposes. In one project in Malawi, no one used their fancy latrines at all. Umelu Chiluzi, a development worker, said, "If you ask them, why are you not using that latrine? They would tell you, 'Are you sure I should put shit in that structure . . . that is even better than my house?'"

Kar realized that open defecation was not a hardware problem, it was a behavioral problem. Until the people in a given area *wanted* to change, the hardware was meaningless.

Acting on this insight, he developed a methodology called Community-Led Total Sanitation (CLTS), which has since been used in more than 60 countries around the world. But don't let the boring acronym fool you: This is a *shocking* process. Here's a stylized description of a typical intervention:

A CLTS facilitator arrives in a village and introduces himself. "I'm studying the sanitation profiles of different villages in the area," he says. "Mind if I look around and ask some questions?" Once he has hung around long enough to attract a small crowd, he conducts a "transect walk," leading the crowd from one side of the village to the other.

"Where do people shit?" he asks, and the villagers direct

him to the common areas of defecation. They are embarrassed, eager to move on, but he lingers. He points: "Whose shit is this?" He asks them, "Did anyone shit here today?" A few hands go up.

The stench is overpowering. People are covering their noses with their clothes. The facilitator keeps asking disgusting questions: "Why is this shit yellow? Why is this one brown?"

The facilitator draws attention to the flies flitting between piles. "Are there often flies here?" Nods all around. He sees a chicken pecking at the shit. "Do you eat this kind of chicken?" More reluctant nods. All his questions are studiously neutral. The facilitator has been trained only to ask questions, not to offer advice or opinions.

The group completes the transect walk and stops in a large public space. The crowd has grown larger, curious about what's happening. The facilitator asks them to draw a rough map of the village in the dirt. Quickly, the villagers map out the boundaries of the village, along with important landmarks—a school, a church, a stream. Then the facilitator asks them to use stones or leaves to mark where their individual homes are.

Once the map has been filled in, he points to a bag of yellow chalk he has brought and asks them to sprinkle some on the places where people shit. He says, "Where there's more shit, use more chalk." There is nervous laughter. The kids enjoy sprinkling the chalk on the open defecation areas.

Now the facilitator asks, "Where do you shit in an emergency—say if there's a rainstorm, or if you have diarrhea?" More laughter as new heaps of yellow chalk are scattered around. Often it circles people's homes—in those emergency situations, people can't make it to the common areas.

It is hard to miss, at this point, that the entire village is covered in yellow.

There is a turbulent energy in the crowd: anxious, disgusted, angry, and embarrassed. They aren't sure what it all means.

The facilitator asks for a glass of water.

Someone provides the water, and he asks a woman if she would feel comfortable drinking it, and she says yes. He asks others and they agree.

He pulls a hair from his head. "What's in my hand?" *A hair.* "Can you see it clearly?" *No, not really.* He walks over to a pile of shit near the meeting area and dips his hair into it. Then he plunges the dirty hair into the glass of water and swirls it around.

He hands the glass to a villager and asks him to take a drink. The man refuses. He passes it along, but they all refuse. "Why do you refuse?" *Because it has shit in it!*

The facilitator looks puzzled. He asks, "How many legs does a fly have?" *Six.* "Right, and they're all serrated. Do you think flies pick up more or less shit than my hair?" *More.*

"Do you ever see flies on your food?" *Yes.* "Then do you throw out the food?" *No.* "Then what are you eating?"

The tension is unbearable now. This is what Kamal Kar calls the "ignition moment." The truth is inescapable: They have been eating each other's shit. For years.

Often at this point, the discussion spirals out of the facilitator's control. People are agitated. They start challenging each other: *We can't continue this! This is madness! How can we stop this?*

They often ask the facilitator what they should do. But he declines to answer. "You know your village better than I do. You're free to choose anything you want, including continuing to defecate in public." But the villagers are determined now. It feels intolerable to live with the status quo another day.

Kar, the inventor of CLTS, knows it is an emotionally wrenching process. "Disgust is the number one trigger," he said. "And shame. 'What the hell are we doing? Are we human beings? Eating each other's shit!'"

CLTS is brutal, and it is effective. Thousands of communities worldwide have declared themselves open-defecation-free (ODF) as a result of the intervention, and in Bangladesh, where CLTS became a cornerstone of national sanitation work, the rate of open defecation has declined from 34% to 1%.

What's odd is that CLTS is not really introducing any "news." In the example above, for instance, people in the village defecated in public every day. They saw their neighbors doing the same. They smelled shit. They stepped over it. They saw the flies, the chickens. Why did the villagers need CLTS to realize something that was right in front of them?

Kar said that villagers will often tell him, "This a truth which nobody wanted to discuss. We're always pushing it under the carpet—and then it was brought out in public and into the daylight. . . . Now there's no way out. The naked truth is out."

They didn't really "see" the truth until they were made to trip over it.

2.

Tripping over the truth is an insight that packs an emotional wallop. When you have a sudden realization, one that you didn't see coming, and one that you know viscerally is right, you've tripped over the truth. It's a defining moment that in an instant can change the way you see the world.

The psychologist Roy Baumeister has studied these kinds of sudden realizations: people who joined and then left a cult, alcoholics who became sober, intellectuals who embraced communism and then recanted. Baumeister said that such situations were often characterized by a "crystallization of discontent," a dramatic moment when an array of isolated misgivings and complaints became linked in a global pattern. Imagine a husband who has a ferocious outburst of temper, and in that moment, his wife realizes that his outbursts aren't just "bad days," as she's always written them off, but a defining character trait. And a trait that she can no longer abide. That's the crystallization of discontent.

Ex–cult members tend to recall a specific moment when their bubble burst, when they could no longer sustain an elevated view of their cult's leader. Baumeister said that their stories reveal that "they had indeed suspected the truth all along but had held their doubts in check, until a focal incident made them see the broad pattern."

The crystallization moments studied by Baumeister are serendipitous. There's no predicting when (or if) they will happen. Notice, though, that the realization sparked by CLTS is very similar in character. Because of the facilitators' questions, people in the villages are made to "see" what had been in front of their eyes the whole time. And that's not a serendipitous "aha!" moment, it's an *engineered* moment.

How do we engineer powerful insights in more ordinary organizational situations? Consider the way Scott Guthrie handled a situation at Microsoft in 2011. He'd been tapped by Steve Ballmer to lead the company's fast-growing cloud computing service, called Azure. Guthrie visited Azure customers, and their feedback about their experience with the service was clear: Azure's underlying technology was good, but it was hard to use. Guthrie knew Azure would never meet its growth expectations until it was much more customer-friendly. But how could he get his colleagues to understand, viscerally, how far off track they were?

He called an off-site meeting with his senior managers and software architects, and he gave them a challenge: Build an app using Azure, just as one of their customers might. It wasn't supposed to be a difficult challenge. But the team struggled. Some execs couldn't use certain features; others couldn't even figure out how to sign up. Guthrie told *Fortune*'s Andrew Nusca, "It was a complete disaster." Chastened, the executives resolved to fix the problems they'd encountered. By the end of their second day, they had produced a plan to completely rebuild Azure.

The Microsoft story and Kamal Kar's story have power for similar reasons. First, the leader knows what truth he wants to share. Guthrie's truth: *Our customers can't use our product.* Kar's: *These villagers are making themselves sick.* Second, the realization strikes fast. It takes minutes or hours, not weeks or months. Tripping happens quickly.

Finally, people in the audience discover the truth for themselves. In turn, that discovery makes the need for action obvious. Guthrie doesn't *share his findings* from his customer meetings; he creates a situation where they can *replicate his discovery*. It becomes their own insight, and as a result, they're motivated to act. Similarly, CLTS facilitators see the problem vividly, but they don't share their concerns directly. They let the villagers see for themselves. The "aha!" moment should always happen in the minds of the audience.

This three-part recipe—a (1) clear insight (2) compressed in time and (3) discovered by the audience itself—provides a blueprint for us when we want people to confront uncomfortable truths. It would have been so easy for CLTS facilitators to lecture the villagers, to show them facts and data about sanitation practices. But it's so much more powerful when the crystallizing insight happens inside them.

3.

To trip is to catch one's foot on something and stumble. To trip over the truth is to catch one's brain on something and struggle. What exactly is the "something" that your brain catches on?

Imagine that you have a good idea that you want other people to support. What would you do? You'd try to sell them on it: *I've explored a lot of different ideas, and this is the best one, because it's supported by a mountain of evidence, and other people who have embraced similar ideas have profited immensely, and did I mention that it's incredibly easy to implement?*

Your focus, in other words, would be on the virtues of the *solution*. But in the stories we've seen so far in this chapter, you'll notice that no one is talking about solutions. Kamal Kar did not tout the virtues of latrines. Microsoft's Scott Guthrie did not pitch a new feature set for Azure.

What they did, instead, was dramatize the *problems:* Ingesting feces. Struggling to use a software package. And once those problems became vivid in the minds of the audience members, their thoughts immediately turned to . . . solutions.

You can't appreciate the solution until you appreciate the problem. So when we talk about "tripping over the truth," we mean *the truth about a problem or harm*. That's what sparks sudden insight.

Honoring this principle requires us to try a new method of persuasion. Take the example of Michael Palmer, an associate professor of chemistry at the University of Virginia and also the associate director of the university's Teaching Resource Center. In 2009, he started a weeklong program called the Course Design Institute (CDI). He created the CDI to help professors design the courses they'd be teaching. On Monday morning, the professors bring in their draft syllabi, and by Friday afternoon, they've overhauled them and created an improved game plan for their courses.

"The dirty secret of higher education is that faculty aren't taught how to teach," said Palmer. Over the course of the week at Palmer's CDI, the professors learn the *science* of teaching: how to motivate students, how to reach different types of learners, and how to ensure that students retain the most important concepts.

A central element of Palmer's approach to planning a course is called "backward-integrated design." First, you identify your goals. Second, you figure out how you'd assess whether students had hit those goals. Third, you design activities that would prepare students to excel at those assessments.

Sounds simple, no doubt. But the life of a college professor makes this kind of planning very counterintuitive. What typically happens to a professor is this: You're assigned to teach a course, often with very little notice before the semester. Let's say it's "Intro to Chemistry I." You flip through a textbook and experience a shock: How in the world can I get through all this material in one semester? It's overwhelming.

There are too many variables to consider all at once, so you put a stake in the ground. You pick a textbook. Now at least you've got a table of contents to use as a rough road map. That's comforting. So you start mapping the chapters to the 14 weeks in your semester. Then, for each week, you can subdivide the topics into lectures. Finally, based on the topics you'll lecture on, you decide what will be on the students' exams.

That may sound like a logical process, but it bears no resemblance to "backward-integrated design." Instead of starting with your goals and working backward, you started with no goals at all! You simply took a big pile of content and subdivided it into class-sized chunks.

Now put yourself in Palmer's shoes. He knows professors are approaching curriculum design the wrong way, and he has a solution for them (backward-integrated design). If he pitched the virtues of the solution, that would make him, in essence, a salesman for backward-integrated design. But how do audiences respond to sales pitches? With skepticism. We quibble and challenge and question.

If Palmer wants to persuade the professors, he needs them to trip over the truth. And that starts with a focus on the problem, not the solution.

On the afternoon of the first day of the Course Design Institute, Palmer introduces an activity called the "Dream Exercise," inspired by an idea in L. Dee Fink's book *Creating Significant Learning Experiences*.

He puts the following question to his audience of 25 to 30 professors: "Imagine that you have a group of dream students. They are engaged, they are perfectly behaved, and they have perfect memories. . . . Fill in this sentence: 3–5 years from now, my students still know _____. Or they still are able to do _____. Or they still find value in _____."

The professors brainstorm privately for about 10 minutes, and then they share their answers. At the CDI in July 2015, a professor who taught an animal behavior course said, "I want them to know the scientific process. If they see some animal doing something interesting, they can come up with a way to work through the scientific process to study it."

A health sciences professor said, "I want them to be connecting and collaborating with colleagues. They will feel confident reviewing new research and being part of 'journal club' meetings."

A math professor said, "I want them to think of math as fun and interesting in its own right, not just practical. . . . When they see a link to a math story, I want them to click it."

Palmer scrawls their answers on a whiteboard at the front of the room. Everyone catches on immediately to one pattern: Very few of the answers are content focused. The math teacher, for instance, did not say he wanted his students to remember the Chain Rule; he said he wanted them to retain a natural interest in math.

Now Palmer is ready to help them trip over the truth. He reminds them that they've just written down their top goals for their students. Then he asks them to pull out the syllabus they brought to the institute. *How much of your current syllabus will advance your students toward the dreams you have for them?*

There's an awkward silence in the room. George Christ, a biomedical engineering professor, remembered the moment with a chuckle: "You look at your syllabus, and you go, 'Zero.'" Most professors discover exactly the same thing. It's a head-slapper of a moment.

Deborah Lawrence, an environmental sciences professor, said, "I quickly realized that the syllabus was useless to me—it wasn't covering any of my objectives."

Palmer's Dream Exercise is a brilliantly designed moment that compels professors to trip over the truth. Their own truth.

The differences between the "before and after" syllabi from the CDI are often striking. (To see an example of a complete syllabus before and after the CDI, visit http://www.heathbroth ers.com/CDIsyllabi.) One physics syllabus, which began as a perfunctory overview of the topics and subtopics in the course, transformed into something inspiring. These are its opening paragraphs:

Why do bridges and buildings stay up? Why do bridges and buildings fall down? How should buildings be built in an earthquake or a hurricane zone? What are some of the forces that bring them down? What is a force?

Physics can describe everything that we see around us, when we know how to look! An airplane flying is a study in pressure and drag; a collision turns into a problem in momentum; a rainbow becomes an awesome show of refraction and dispersion; an earthquake illustrates shear forces and flexibility; bridge construction is about heat and expansion; a concert hall is the interplay of reflection and interference.

This class will give you the tools with which to approach these and many more exciting problems relevant to your world. Training yourselves as physicists, you will see the world as a complex interplay of forces and principles. You will learn and understand fundamental principles of physics.

From 2008 to 2015, 295 instructors participated in the Course Design Institute. They rated the experience 4.76 out of 5.0. All 295 of them—not one exception—said they'd recommend the course to a colleague.

One instructor from 2011 wrote, "In two words, it was life altering. This may seem overblown, but it is 100% true. I came in thinking I had a handle on my course, but realized very soon I needed go back to the drawing board. The result is exponentially improved."

Bear in mind that professors are not prone to strong emotional reactions. The Course Design Institute provides the motivational jolt and concrete direction they need to revamp their courses.

Sometimes, in life, we can't get our bearings until we trip over the truth.

6

Stretch for Insight

1.

Lea Chadwell had been baking for only a year when she began to daydream about starting her own company.

In her day job, she worked at an animal hospital—the same place she'd once brought her dogs for medical treatment. After visiting a few times as a customer, she realized: *I want to work here.* She begged for a job, and four months later, a role as a vet tech opened up.

Nine years later, though, she felt like she'd maxed out the pay raises and promotions available to her. She also worried it was a young person's job. "Am I really going to be wrestling golden retrievers when I'm 65?" she wondered.

She spent every weekend in the kitchen, making Swedish cookies, pastries with exotic spices, flavored brioches. Friends and family started telling her, "You should have your own bakery!" (Which is the kind of advice you give when you expect free samples down the road.)

One day in 2006, her husband, Sam, heard a story on the radio about a business that allowed you to "test-drive" your dream job. For a fee, Vocation Vacations could arrange for you to spend a few days shadowing people who were living your dream. The jobs available for visit included cattle ranching, managing a bed-and-breakfast, owning a winery, and—there it was!—starting a bakery.*

Chadwell jumped at the opportunity, flying to Portland, Oregon, to work with the owners of a bakery and chocolate shop. It was like being able to rent a mentor. She loved it and returned home determined to start her own bakery.

She took classes at night to refine her skills, eventually earning a certificate from a local culinary program. In 2010, she was ready: She opened A Pound of Butter. She made custom cakes for birthdays and weddings and supplied pastries to local restaurants, working evenings and weekends while she kept her job at the animal hospital. Eventually, she planned to open a full retail shop. "I would daydream about how the bakery would be," she said. "I thought that would be something I could do for the rest of my days."

Carved cakes were her specialty—Chadwell had majored in sculpture in college. She conjured impeccable Thomas the Tank Engine cakes and Disney princess cakes for kids' birthday parties.

---

* Vocation Vacations has since become Pivot Planet, with a focus on calls rather than in-person visits.

Slowly, though, the charm started to fade. Baking cakes for her own family was fun. But baking cakes for demanding customers was stressful. She treated sick animals by day and handled nervous brides at night. She felt stuck in an endless cycle. "I needed more business so that I could afford the bakery, but I didn't have time to bake, because I couldn't afford to live on the bakery," she said.

One weekend, racing against a deadline, she finished putting the last touches on a buttercream wedding cake and loaded it into her car. Just as she prepared to drive off, she realized she was about to leave the front door of her unoccupied bakery wide open.

It was her lightning-bolt moment: *I'm making myself crazy being this stressed out.* And she realized, "I wasn't in love with baking anymore," she said later. "It was like this albatross of butter around my neck."

She was almost 42 and she wanted one career, not two. She saw it in a flash: "If I do this 'right,' and get loans, and have a storefront, I will never come back from this if it fails. I will never financially recover. . . . I'm not passionate about this enough anymore."

She folded A Pound of Butter after about 18 months. Her bakery-owner fantasy was over.

She didn't bake a cake for years afterward.

This is not the ending we crave. We want likable entrepreneurs to succeed. We want daydreams to come true.

Did Lea Chadwell fail? In some ways, yes. But it's not quite that simple. Chadwell doesn't regret starting her bakery, and she doesn't regret closing it. What she gained was the insight that comes from experience. She came to accept, she said, some qualities that made her the wrong person to run her own business. "I'm unorganized. Impractical. Fickle. . . . While these traits make me a great candidate for a Wacky Friend, they are just awful to try to form a business around. I suspect if I hadn't quit, I'd have failed, and it actually really sucks to admit it. But, there's the painful lesson I've learned. I'm great when I'm working for others; they rely on me. Working for myself? I'm a terrible boss."

Psychologists call this "self-insight"—a mature understanding of our capabilities and motivations—and it's correlated with an array of positive outcomes, ranging from good relationships to a sense of purpose in life. Self-insight and psychological well-being go together.

Chadwell's self-insight was sparked by a classic "crystallization of discontent" moment—the moment when she almost drove away from her bakery with the door wide open. In an instant, the fragments of frustration and anxiety she'd experienced were assembled into a clear conclusion: *I'm not good at this. It's not me.*

Compare Chadwell's moment with a second one experienced by a woman who, in college, decided to study abroad in Rome. "I was a small town girl, terrified of things like public transport as well as the daunting task of working in an environment where people did not speak my language," she said. "I remember arriving and the whole place overwhelming me. . . . "

Four weeks later, she had convinced a shop worker that she was Italian. (She blew her cover, unfortunately, when she couldn't come up with the Italian word for "hair tie.") By the end of the experience, she had transformed. "I came back different," she said. "I was far more confident and far more willing to take calculated risks. . . . I became unafraid of travelling or living anywhere else." She lives in London now.

Her defining moment—convincing the shop worker that she was a "native"—is almost the mirror image of Chadwell's. She realized: *I can do this. I can be this person.*

Both women experienced moments of self-insight sparked by "stretching." To stretch is to place ourselves in situations that expose us to the risk of failure.

What may be counterintuitive is that self-insight rarely comes from staying in our heads. Research suggests that *reflecting* or *ruminating* on our thoughts and feelings is an ineffective way to achieve true understanding. Studying our own *behavior* is more fruitful.

"Wouldn't I make a fabulous bakery owner?" "Could I hack it in Italy?" These are important questions but impossible to answer in one's head. Better to take a risk, try something, and distill the answer from experience rather than from navel-gazing. Action leads to insight more often than insight leads to action.

Learning who we are, and what we want, and what we're capable of—it's a lifelong process. Let's face it: Many of us became adults—with homes and jobs and spouses—long before we really understood ourselves. Why do we react the way we do? What are our blind spots? Why are we attracted to the kind of friends and lovers that we seek out?

Self-understanding comes slowly. One of the few ways to

accelerate it—to experience more crystallizing moments—is
to stretch for insight.

2.

In the spring of 1984, Michael Dinneen was serving the last
night of his psychiatry rotation at Naval Medical Center San
Diego. He had completed medical school in 1982 and was in
the second year of his residency training, which would allow
him to become a fully certified psychiatrist.

The patients on the psych ward had serious illnesses—
schizophrenia, bipolar disorder, depression—and most of them
were in locked rooms. Many had tried to hurt themselves or
others in the past. As Dinneen made his rounds, he encountered a patient who had earned the freedom to walk around on
his own. The man was scheduled for discharge the next day.

He stopped Dinneen and said, "I have some things I'd like
to ask you."

Dinneen replied, "I've got some things to take care of, can I
come back in 15 minutes?" The patient nodded, and Dinneen
continued with his rounds.

Ten minutes later, a "code blue" call came over the in-
tercom, meaning a patient needed resuscitation. Typically the
announcement directed staffers to a specific floor and room
within the hospital. But this time it directed them to the exte-
rior courtyard. Dinneen rushed outside.

Sprawled on the ground was the patient he'd just spoken

to. The man had jumped from the third-floor balcony onto the concrete walkway. Dinneen and other staffers sped to his side and tried to resuscitate him. When he didn't respond, they rushed him to the ER. He died shortly thereafter.

Dinneen walked slowly back toward his office in the psych ward. He was shocked and racked with guilt. *I'm a complete failure*, he thought. *I should have known he needed me.*

He called the residency training director, Richard Ridenour, to report on what had happened, and took some time to comfort the staff of the psych ward. Exhausted, he prepared to go home, feeling emotionally unable to finish out his shift.

In the meantime, Ridenour had arrived at the hospital. He asked Dinneen to go over the whole story again. "My full expectation after giving that report," said Dinneen, "was that it would be used for disciplinary action." Having a patient commit suicide was rare; having one commit suicide in the apparent safe haven of the hospital was even rarer. Dinneen was not sure he'd be allowed to practice anymore.

Instead, Ridenour said, "Okay, let's get back to work."

He led Dinneen to the operating room, where they picked out some clean scrubs and a white coat. Then they returned to the psych ward.

And Ridenour, his mentor, stayed with him the whole night.

In recalling the episode later, Ridenour said, "I didn't want to send a message to Mike that he had done something wrong. I wanted to send a message to him that he was fine. Let's move on. It's kind of like death in combat. Patients die on the triage table, you go on. There are other patients who are waiting in the wings. Maybe you can save them."

Dinneen said, "I don't remember much from the rest of the night, but I do know that if I had gone home, I might have given up on becoming a psychiatrist."

More than thirty years later, Michael Dinneen looks back on that night as one of the defining moments of his life. It was the first time he had lost a patient. But what sticks with him nearly as much is what the night taught him about himself: *I can endure.*

In Dinneen's life, the episode was a negative peak (a pit). Barbara Fredrickson, one of the researchers who pioneered the "peak-end principle," argued that the reason we over-weight peaks in memory is that they serve as a kind of psychic price tag. They tell us, in essence, *this is what it could cost you to endure that experience again.* Some people, like Lea Chadwell, discover that the cost is too high, and they choose to avoid facing those moments again. Others, like Dinneen, discover that they can survive the experiences, and that the potential negative peaks are outweighed by the positive.

Note the other big difference between the stories of Chadwell and Dinneen. Dinneen never would have learned about his ability to endure had he not been pushed and supported by Ridenour. "I was expected to get back in the game," said Dinneen. "He knew I had it in me to make it through that night when I didn't know that myself." Ridenour's wise actions in the middle of the night transformed a moment of trauma into a moment of growth.

Often it's other people who prod us to stretch. You hire

a personal trainer because you know she's going to push you beyond your comfort zone. And this is the same quality we value about our mentors: They bring out the best in us. You'll never hear someone say, "Yeah, the best coach I ever had was Coach Martin. He had no expectations whatsoever and let us do whatever we wanted. He was a great man."

Mentors focus on improvement: Can you push a little bit further? Can you shoulder a little more responsibility? They introduce a productive level of stress.

To explore that idea, we gave some of our readers a challenge: Encourage someone whom you mentor to stretch. Jim Honig, a Lutheran pastor, reported giving his pastoral intern a challenge: "One of the highlights of the year is our Easter Vigil service on the night before Easter Sunday morning. I usually don't schedule an intern to preach that service, usually choosing to do that myself. This year, I told the intern that he would be preaching at that service. I told him that it was an important service and that he needed to bring his best, but that I was sure he could do it."

Pastor Honig admitted he was hesitant about delegating such an important service. But the intern responded: He delivered one of his best sermons, Honig said.

What are the "defining moments" in this situation? There are two. The first was the intern's sermon at the Easter Vigil service. That's a moment of elevation (raised stakes), pride, and insight (*I can handle this*). It was a moment created (or enabled) by Pastor Honig's push. But Pastor Honig also stretched! He made himself vulnerable; he risked failure by trusting an intern with such an important moment. And as a result of taking that risk, he gained insight. "The rest of the staff knows how particular I am about the preaching task during Holy Week and Easter. So, they were surprised when I let others take some of the preaching load that week. They all rose to the occasion. It also gave me pause to reflect on how I might make that more of my practice. It's something I've been working on and we are reaping the benefits."

3.

Mentors push, mentees stretch. If you mentor someone—a student, an employee, a relative—you might wonder about the best way to give them a productive push. A good starting place is a two-part formula cited in a paper by the psychologist David Scott Yeager and eight colleagues: high standards + assurance.

Yeager described a study in a suburban junior high school in which 44 seventh-grade students were assigned to write an essay about a personal hero. Their teachers then marked up the essays, providing written feedback.

At that point, the researchers collected the papers from the teachers and split the essays randomly into two piles. They appended a generic note, in the teacher's handwriting, to each essay in the first pile. It said, "I'm giving you these comments so that you'll have feedback on your paper." The essays in the second pile got a note reflecting what the researchers call "wise criticism." It said, "I'm giving you these comments because I have very high expectations and I know you can reach them." (High standards + assurance.)

After the papers were returned, the students had the option to revise and resubmit their paper in the hopes of earning a better grade. About 40% of the students who got the generic note chose to revise their papers. But almost 80% of the wise criticism students revised their papers, and in editing their papers, they made more than twice as many corrections as the other students.

What makes the second note so powerful is that it rewires the way students process criticism. When they get their paper back, full of corrections and suggestions, their natural reaction might be defensiveness or even mistrust. *The teacher has never liked me.* But the wise criticism note carries a different message. It says, *I know you're capable of great things if you'll just put in the work.* The marked-up essay is not a personal judgment. It's a push to stretch.

4.

In organizations, mentorship can take a stronger form. *High standards + assurance* is a powerful formula, but ultimately it's just a statement of expectations. What great mentors do is add two more elements: direction and support. *I have high expectations for you and I know you can meet them. So try this new challenge and if you fail, I'll help you recover.* That's mentorship in two sentences. It sounds simple, yet it's powerful enough to transform careers.

In 2015, Dale Phelps was the director of Quality, Service,

and Service Operations for Cummins Northeast, a distributor for Cummins products. Translation: Say you've got a contract to build a bunch of city buses for Boston, and you decide to use diesel engines made by Cummins. In that case, Cummins Northeast will process your order, deliver the engines, and provide service if they break down. Phelps's job was to find ways to make the company's service better and more efficient.

In doing his work, Phelps relied heavily on the discipline of Six Sigma. If you manufacture products—let's say rubber balls—naturally you want them to be free of defects. A "six sigma" process is one that produces only 3.4 defects per million attempts. So if you make a million rubber balls, only 3 or 4 of them will be warped or lopsided. To achieve that level of excellence, you must obsessively monitor the manufacturing process, gathering data to pinpoint problems and to reduce variability. The people who perform these feats of process improvement are practitioners of Six Sigma, and their voodoo can also be practiced on nonmanufacturing situations as well, such as reducing surgical errors or, in the case of Phelps, speeding up engine repair. The most talented practitioners seek out certification as a Six Sigma Black Belt, an honorific that has nothing to do with karate but rather reflects a noble and ultimately hopeless attempt to give the work some sex appeal.

Back to the story: Phelps needed a Six Sigma Black Belt to assist him with his work in Albany, New York, and he hired Ranjani Sreenivasan for the role. Raised in India, Sreenivasan had been in the United States for only three years, having come to complete her master's degree in mechanical engineering.

Sreenivasan's role was to use Six Sigma to help colleagues improve their processes, for instance by reorganizing the service shops so that more frequently used tools were closer at hand. But she struggled in the role. "She was kind of shy, a little withdrawn," said Phelps. He worried that she wasn't assertive enough to be taken seriously by the experienced hands at the firm.

Sreenivasan had a different perspective. She wasn't introverted—her friends had nicknamed her "Thunder," because they always knew when she was in the room. Rather, she was overwhelmed. She knew a lot about Six Sigma but almost nothing about servicing diesel engines. In meetings she felt as if her colleagues were "speaking in Greek and Latin." She'd take notes of all the terms they used and ask someone later what they meant.

At her first team meeting for a Six Sigma project, she sat silently, and afterward approached Phelps, distraught. "I was so upset," she said. "I was seen as this new hire who knew nothing."

There was grumbling about her performance. Phelps knew she was the right person for the job, but she was in jeopardy. So he gave her a push. Phelps challenged her to get out in the field and spend some time learning the business. Until she could speak the insiders' language, it would be difficult for her to command respect.

"I was a little apprehensive," Sreenivasan said. Visiting the field meant leaving the safety of her own expertise, which was data and spreadsheets. She worried about exposing her lack of knowledge to her colleagues. Plus, she was young (24), female, and Indian, all three of which were uncommon in the company.

Her first field visit was to the branch in Rocky Hill, Connecticut. The manager of the branch, one of the few women at that level of leadership, showed her around and tutored her on the business. Sreenivasan stayed for a week and came back to Albany energized.

"That visit was a game changer," she said. "All the operational terms started to become clear. Charlene [the Rocky Hill leader] told me how proud she was that I was doing so much at such a young age."

Phelps lined up additional field visits, and Sreenivasan became more and more comfortable sharing her Six Sigma insights. Phelps started to hear back from his colleagues how impressed they were. Some of the people who had grumbled about her performance were now citing her as one of their top performers.

"I learned that I'm capable of more than I thought," she said. "I didn't know I could be an operations kind of person. I thought I was a data person. . . . I didn't have the confidence in myself that Dale had in me."

Phelps blames himself for her early difficulties. "I tried to insulate her from a lot of stuff, which in hindsight wasn't effective and really wasn't fair to her. If you're always in a life vest, you don't know if you can swim. Sometimes you have to take the life vest off—with someone still standing by to offer support and rescue—and say, 'Let's see what happens.'"

This story captures the "formula" for mentorship that we've been exploring:

High standards + assurance

("I specifically told her that I had high expectations for what I thought she could accomplish," Phelps said.)

+ Direction + support

(Phelps suggested the field visits to correct the perceived "hole" in her experience and ensured that her first visit was with a female leader.)

= Enhanced self-insight.

(Sreenivasan: "I learned that I'm capable of more than I thought. . . . I didn't know I could be an operations kind of person.")

5.

A mentor's push leads to a stretch, which creates a moment of self-insight. What can be counterintuitive about this vision of mentorship is the part about pushing. It requires the mentor to expose the mentee to risk. That can be unnatural; our instinct with the people we care about is to *protect them from risk*. To insulate them.

This is also a classic tension of parenting, of course: Should you give your kids the freedom to make mistakes, or should you shield them? Most parents tiptoe nervously along the line between under- and overprotectiveness.

How do you encourage your kids to stretch—but not too far? Consider the story of Sara Blakely, a woman who was raised to stretch. Blakely is the founder of Spanx, whose first product—basically a comfortable girdle—was an instant hit.* The founding story has become a legend: In 1998, Blakely was getting dressed for a party and she decided to wear her new pair of fitted white pants. But she faced a dilemma. She wanted to wear pantyhose underneath for their slimming effect, but she also wanted bare feet so she could wear sandals. Should she wear hose or not?

Inspiration struck: She cut the feet off her hose and wore them to the party. Her innovation had its problems—the severed ends of the hose kept rolling up her legs—but she thought to herself, *This is my chance. I'll create a better version of this product, and women will love it.*

Two years later, in 2000, she signed up her first client for Spanx, Neiman Marcus, and Oprah chose Spanx as one of her "Favorite Things." Twelve years later, *Forbes* named Blakely the youngest self-made female billionaire in history.

In *Getting There: A Book of Mentors,* Blakely wrote, "I can't tell you how many women come up to me and say something like 'I've been cutting the feet out of my pantyhose for years. Why didn't I end up being the Spanx girl?' The reason is that a good idea is just a starting point."

What separated Blakely from other women with the same idea was her persistence. In the early days of Spanx she heard constantly that her idea was stupid or silly. In one meeting with

---

* Just wanted you to know that we resisted the urge to include a cheap joke about Spanx in the "Stretch" chapter.

a law firm, she noticed that one of the lawyers kept looking around the room, suspiciously. Later, the lawyer confessed to her, "Sara, I thought when I first met you that your idea was so bad that I thought you had been sent by *Candid Camera.*"

Men were largely incapable of understanding the genius of her idea, and unfortunately men held most of the positions she needed to influence to get the product made. (She tried, in vain, to find one female patent lawyer in the state of Georgia.) The owners of textile mills — men, all — rejected her idea again and again. She was only able to create a prototype of the product when one mill owner shared the idea with his daughters — who insisted that he call her back.

What equipped her to survive this gauntlet of failure? Blakely's previous job had been selling fax machines. When she started that job, she didn't receive a lead sheet of people interested in owning a fax machine. Instead her supervisor gave her a territory of four zip codes and handed her a phone book for "leads."

"I would wake up in the morning and drive around cold-calling from eight until five," she wrote. "Most doors were slammed in my face. I saw my business card ripped up at least once a week, and I even had a few police escorts out of buildings. It wasn't long before I grew immune to the word 'no' and even found my situation amusing."

That's a powerful moment of insight. She realizes: *I don't fear failure anymore. It's no longer an obstacle to me.*

Blakely had been selling fax machines for *seven years* when she attended the party in her white pants and had her Spanx epiphany. Her relentlessness in building Spanx came from enduring seven years' worth of—mostly—failure. (To be clear, she was very successful as fax salespeople go.)

What's the source of Blakely's extraordinary grit? It was incubated, no doubt, by her time in sales. But there was something else in her background as well. When Blakely and her brother were growing up, her father would ask them a question every week at the dinner table: "What did you guys fail at this week?"

"If we had nothing to tell him, he'd be disappointed," Blakely said. "The logic seems counterintuitive, but it worked beautifully. He knew that many people become paralyzed by the fear of failure. They're constantly afraid of what others will think if they don't do a great job and, as a result, take no risks. My father wanted us to try everything and feel free to push the envelope. His attitude taught me to define failure as not try-ing something I want to do instead of not achieving the right outcome."

His question, "What did you guys fail at this week?" was a push to stretch. It was an attempt to normalize failure, to make it part of a casual dinner conversation. Because when you seek out situations where you might fail, failure loses some of its menace. You've been inoculated against it.

Mr. Blakely's daughter Sara internalized the meaning of that dinner-table question more than he ever could have imag-ined.

That's the story ending that we crave: A likable entrepreneur, inspired by her father, lives her dream and is richly rewarded by the world. Some entrepreneurs win, some entrepreneurs lose. What they share is a willingness to put themselves in a situation where they *can* fail. It's always safer to stay put—you can't stumble when you stand still.

This is familiar advice for anyone who has ever browsed a self-help aisle of books. Get out there! Try something different! Turn over a new leaf! Take a risk! In general, this seems like sound advice, especially for people who feel stuck. But one note of caution: The advice often seems to carry a whispered promise of success. Take a risk and you'll succeed! Take a risk and you'll like the New You better!

That's not quite right. A risk is a risk. Lea Chadwell took a risk on a bakery; it made her miserable. If risks always paid off, they wouldn't be risks.

The promise of stretching is not success, it's learning. It's self-insight. It's the promise of gleaning the answers to some of the most important and vexing questions of our lives: What do we want? What can we do? Who can we be? What can we endure?

A psychiatric intern learns that he has the strength to endure trauma. A "small-town girl" learns she can thrive in a foreign country. And even those who fail benefit from learning: Chadwell learned more about what she truly values in life.

By stretching, we create moments of self-insight, that wellspring of mental health and well-being.

We will never know our reach unless we stretch.

MOMENTS OF INSIGHT
THE WHIRLWIND REVIEW

1. Moments of insight deliver realizations and transformations.

2. They need not be serendipitous. To deliver moments of insight for others, we can lead them to "trip over the truth," which means sparking a realization that packs an emotional wallop.
   - *Kamal Kar's CLTS causes communities to trip over the truth of open defecation's harms.*

3. Tripping over the truth involves (1) a clear insight (2) compressed in time and (3) discovered by the audience itself.
   - *In the "Dream Exercise," professors discover they're spending no time in class on their most important goals.*

4. To produce moments of *self-insight*, we need to *stretch*: placing ourselves in new situations that expose us to the risk of failure.
   - *Lea Chadwell took a risk by opening a bakery. Overwhelmed, she closed it, and in the process learned more about her capabilities and her values.*

5. Mentors can help us stretch further than we thought we could, and in the process they can spark defining moments.
   - *The psychiatry resident Michael Dinneen had a mentor who pushed him to continue working through the night: "He knew I had it in me to make it through that night when I didn't know that myself."*

6. The formula for mentorship that leads to self-insight: High standards + assurance + direction + support.
   - *Six Sigma expert Ranjani Sreenivasan was pushed by her mentor to develop skills in company operations. "I learned that I'm capable of more than I thought," she said.*

7. Expecting our mentees to stretch requires us to overcome our natural instinct to protect the people we care about from risk. To insulate them.
   - *Spanx founder Sara Blakely's dad: "What did you guys fail at this week?" He wanted to make it easier (less scary) for his kids to stretch.*

8. The promise of stretching is not success, it's learning.

—————————— **Clinic 3** ——————————
Improving a Chinese Restaurant

The situation: Angela Yang is the owner of Panda Garden House, a fairly conventional American Chinese-food restaurant in Raleigh, North Carolina—the kind of place that features General Tso's chicken, wonton soup, and paper Chinese zodiac placemats. In the era of restaurant review apps like Yelp, Angela sees an opportunity for the restaurant, to make a name for itself. She's ready to make some big changes. (Both Angela and the restaurant are fictitious.)

The desire: Yang is proud of the food that the restaurant serves but agrees with many of its reviewers that the customer experience is underwhelming. How can she make eating at Panda Garden House dramatically more interesting and memorable?

How Do We Create a Defining Moment?

What's the moment? Panda Garden House is never going to offer a Michelin-star gourmet experience. But remember the lesson of the Magic Castle and its Popsicle Hotline: Great experiences are mostly forgettable and occasionally remarkable. Angela need not reinvent every part of the experience—she just needs to invest in a few moments of magic.

Add ELEVATION:

1: Boost sensory appeal and break the script. Fancy restaurants will often serve every guest an amuse-bouche, a bite-size appetizer provided for free. What if Panda Garden House offered its customer its own signature starter for free? (A miniature pork dumpling?) Or what if patrons, like first-class airline passengers, were presented before their meals with steaming hot towels, scented with jasmine?

Add INSIGHT:

1: Stretch for insight. The restaurant could feature a dish that allowed you to test your own "spice endurance"—say, a plate that featured the same dish with five escalating levels of heat. You could test your mettle against the spice tolerance of the Chinese. (Note that this could also double as a moment of pride involving "leveling up." See Chapter 8.)

Add PRIDE:

1: Multiply milestones. Eleven Madison Park in New York City, one of the world's most acclaimed restaurants, once challenged diners to take a quiz in which they tasted a variety of chocolates and tried to identify which animal's milk they were made from (cow, goat, sheep, or buffalo). What if Panda Garden House adapted the idea, offering a small sampler of foods from four different regions of China—or using four different common spices—and challenged diners to do the matching? Anyone who nailed all four matches would be awarded a coveted "Big Panda" sticker.

Add CONNECTION:

1: At a table where patrons are drinking alcohol, a waiter could offer to share a few rules of Chinese drinking etiquette. For instance, if you clink glasses with another person, you must drink what's left in your glass. And if you're clinking with an elder or boss, it's respectful to make sure that when you clink, the rim of your glass is below the rim of theirs.

2: Deepen ties. What if Panda Garden House rebranded "fortune cookies" as "friendship cookies" and included provocative questions inside, intended to spark conversation at the table? You might break open your cookie to find: "When did you last sing to yourself? To someone else?"

Final reflections: Just a few of these moments could substantially improve the customer experience. Many of these ideas were suggested by a class of business students; no doubt real restaurateurs would have much better ideas. What we wanted you to see in this Clinic is that it's easy to *generate ideas* for memorable experiences simply by paying attention to the principles you've encountered in this book.

Moments of ELEVATION

Moments of INSIGHT

Moments of PRIDE

Moments of CONNECTION

Introduction to Moments of Pride

Moments of elevation lift us above the everyday. Moments of insight spark discoveries about our world and ourselves. And moments of pride capture us at our best—showing courage, earning recognition, conquering challenges.

How do you make moments of pride? The recipe seems clear: You work hard, you put in the time, and as a result, you get more talented and accomplish more, and those achievements spark pride. Simple as that.

There's a lot of truth to that "roll up your sleeves" advice. But when you start thinking in moments, you notice that the advice misses several important points. First, regardless of how skilled we are, it's usually *having our skill noticed by others* that sparks the moment of pride. If you think about your own moments of pride in your career, our bet is that many of them were examples of *recognition:* You were promoted. You won an award. You were praised. In Chapter 7, we'll see how simple and powerful it can be to create defining moments for others through recognition. We'll also encounter an experience that lasts an hour and elevates your happiness for a month afterward. (And, no, it's not Krispy Kreme.)

What's also true is that two people chasing the same goal—and putting in the same amount of hard work—can experience different amounts of pride, depending on how they choose to structure their work. You'll learn how to "design for pride," using the principles of gaming to multiply the number of defining moments you experience en route to your destination (Chapter 8: "Multiply Milestones"). You'll come to understand, for instance, why so many Americans never hit their goal to "learn Spanish."

Finally, we'll investigate some of people's proudest experiences: moments of courage, moments when they stood up for what they believed in. These moments are not a by-product of hard work; the opportunities to be courageous can arise unexpectedly, and sometimes we kick ourselves later that we didn't act. But we'll see that, just as we can practice physical and intellectual skills, we can practice the moral skill of courage (Chapter 9: "Practice Courage"). We'll study how soldiers get comfortable with defusing bombs and how arachnophobes can make peace with spiders.

In short, hard work is essential, but it doesn't guarantee that we'll experience defining moments. In this section, you'll learn three strategies for living a life rich with pride. So turn the page and transport yourself back to a time that spawns many (negative) defining moments: middle school.

7

Recognize Others

1.

Kira Sloop remembers it as the worst year of her life. It was 1983 and she was entering the sixth grade. "Imagine, if you will, an awkward 11-year-old with a terrible set of teeth, out-of-control curls, and very low self-esteem," she said. Her parents had divorced during the summer prior to the start of school.

The one class she looked forward to was chorus. Sloop had a powerful voice and a "flair for the dramatic," she said. Relatives told her she should be a country singer.

Something happened early in the semester that is still seared into her memory. The students were arranged into groups on the risers: altos, sopranos, tenors, and baritones. The music teacher—"a woman with a beehive-ish hairdo and a seemingly permanent frown on her face"—led the choir in a familiar song, using a pointer to click the rhythm of the song on a music stand.

Then, Sloop remembered, "She started walking over toward me. Listening, leaning in closer. Suddenly she stopped the song and addressed me directly: 'You there. Your voice sounds . . . different . . . and it's not blending in with the other girls at all. Just pretend to sing.'"

The comment crushed her: "The rest of the class snickered, and I wished the floor would open and swallow me up." For the rest of the year, whenever the choir sang, she mouthed the words.

"Chorus was supposed to be my favorite thing," she said. "My family said I could sing, but the teacher said I couldn't. So I started to question everything." She began to act out, hanging out with the wrong crowd at school. It was a dark time.

Then, in the summer after her seventh-grade year, she attended a camp for gifted kids in North Carolina called the Cullowhee Experience. She surprised herself by signing up to participate in chorus. During practice, she mouthed the words, but the teacher noticed what she was doing and asked Sloop to stick around after class.

The teacher was short and thin, with hair down to her waist—a "lovely flower child," said Sloop. She invited Sloop to sit next to her on the piano bench, and they began to sing together in the empty room.

Sloop was hesitant at first but eventually lowered her guard. She said, "We sang scale after scale, song after song, harmonizing and improvising, until we were hoarse."

Then the teacher took Sloop's face in her hands and looked her in the eyes and said: "You have a distinctive, expressive, and beautiful voice. You could have been the love child of Bob Dylan and Joan Baez."

As she left the room that day, she felt as if she'd shed a ton of weight. "I was on top of the world," she said. Then she went to the library to find out who Joan Baez was.

"For the rest of that magical summer," Sloop said, she experienced a metamorphosis, "shedding my cocoon and emerging as a butterfly looking for light." (And, on the heels of her personal defining moment with the teacher came a romantic defining moment with another campmate—see the footnote.)* She became more and more confident in her singing. In high school, she joined the theater department and played the lead in almost every musical production. She grew comfortable in front of audiences until, in her proudest moment, she sang with her choir at Carnegie Hall.

Carnegie Hall! This was the same girl who had once been told to "mouth the words."

---

* During the summer camp, the students took a field trip to Gatlinburg, Tennessee, and at one of the places they visited, there was a "recording booth" where you could sing a famous tune and walk away with your track on a cassette tape. On a lark, Sloop and two friends recorded the Beatles' "I Want to Hold Your Hand," and on the bus ride home to camp, they convinced the bus driver to play it. One boy on the bus listened to the song and loved it, and he remembers it was the first time he'd really noticed Kira. His name was Ross Sloop. Five summer camps, nine years, and one remarkable coincidence later, he would ask Kira to marry him. The remarkable coincidence? After college, Kira was working at a store that provided VHS video rentals. A customer returned a video one day—his name was Ed Slocum. Kira went into the store's customer database to mark the video "returned," and she happened to notice the name directly below Slocum's in the directory: Ross Sloop, her old campmate. She wrote down his phone number (thereby violating several confidential/privacy statutes, no doubt). She called him later. And the rest, as they say, is history.

2.

Sloop's story is moving and inspiring and—here's the biggest surprise—commonplace. The sociologist Gad Yair interviewed 1,100 people about their key educational experiences, and he found that many of them had strikingly similar tales to tell. Here's a story that Yair cites as typical:

> *I was 12 years old; I was regarded by all the teachers as a "weak" student; and school seemed cold and alienating. My teacher went on maternity leave, and the new teacher declared that she ignores past achievements and starts from a clean slate. She gave homework and I did my best to succeed.*
>
> *A day later I read my homework aloud . . . and the new teacher praised my work in front of everybody. I, the "weak" student, the Ugly Duckling of my class, suddenly turned into a beautiful swan. She gave me confidence and opened a new clean page for me for success without ever looking back at my dark prior achievements.*

The similarities with Sloop's story are clear. First, there's a bleak period of alienation and rejection. Then a new teacher appears, offering praise and support. Which leads to a transformation: The Ugly Duckling turns into a beautiful swan.

Yair heard stories like this again and again. He titled his research paper "Cinderellas and Ugly Ducklings: Positive Turning Points in Students' Educational Careers."

Our intention is not to diminish the power of these stories by pointing out their similarities. On the contrary, it's precisely the similarities that illustrate the larger truth: A few minutes can change a life. These moments didn't just happen; thoughtful teachers made them happen.

But how many more defining moments didn't happen because the teachers were tired or distracted or weren't sure how to translate their concern about a student into a meaningful conversation? What if every teacher received guidance about handling students, like Sloop, who seem hurt and withdrawn? It could be included in new teacher training: *Here's what we know about how to make a lasting impact in a child's life in a few precious minutes.*

Of all the ways we can create moments of pride for others, the simplest is to offer them recognition. In this chapter, we'll see why recognizing others is so important, how to handle the moment so that it's most effective, and why the good feelings enjoyed by the recipient can boomerang back to the giver.

3.

Carolyn Wiley of Roosevelt University reviewed four similar studies of employee motivation conducted in 1946, 1980, 1986, and 1992. In each of the studies, employees were asked to rank the factors that motivated them. Popular answers included "interesting work," "job security," "good wages," and "feeling of being in on things." Across the studies, which spanned 46 years, only one factor was cited every time as among the top two motivators: "full appreciation of work done."

The importance of recognition to employees is inarguable. But here's the problem: While recognition is a universal expectation, it's not a universal *practice*.

Wiley sums up the research: "More than 80 per cent of supervisors claim they frequently express appreciation to their subordinates, while less than 20 per cent of the employees report that their supervisors express appreciation more than occasionally." Call it the recognition gap.

This gap has consequences: One survey found that the top reason people leave their jobs is a lack of praise and recognition. Corporate leaders are aware of this inadequacy, and their response has generally been to create recognition *programs*, like Employee of the Month awards or annual banquets recognizing star performers. But these programs are inadequate for two reasons. First, the scale is all wrong. When we talk about the need to recognize employees, we're not aiming for one employee per month! The proper pace of recognition is weekly or even daily, not monthly or yearly.

Second, the mulish formality of the program can breed cynicism. For example, every Employee of the Month program in human history has been plagued by a similar dynamic: If you judged the award fairly, your best employee would win the award every month, but it seems socially awkward to give it to Jenny every time, so you start concocting reasons to spread the award around, and after a year or two of hopscotching among employees, Stuart is the only guy on the team who hasn't won, and it's becoming An Issue, so one November you throw him a bone ("He has made real progress on his tardiness!"), and from that moment on, anytime you say the phrase "Employee of the Month," your employees will roll their eyes. And pray it's not them.*

Recognition experts have advice on how to escape this trap. For formal recognition programs, they recommend using objective measurements, such as sales volume, to protect against cynicism. If Stuart doesn't hit the sales target, he won't win the award, period.

The larger point is that most recognition should be personal, not programmatic. In our own research, when we asked people about the defining moments in their careers, we were struck by how often they cited simple, personal events. Here's one example:

> I was greatly commended by my manager for prepping the backroom by cleaning and reorganizing all the bikes for easy scanning for inventory. I felt proud that someone actually took the time to acknowledge my effort. . . .

And here's another:

> A few years ago, I was working in the office when a new client to work with came in. He seemed to be in a bad

---

* Great *Simpsons* moment: Homer is the only employee of the power plant not to have won the "Worker of the Week Award." Mr. Burns, the owner of the power plant, has called his employees together to announce the week's winner: "I can't believe we've overlooked this week's winner for so very long." In the audience, Homer smiles and fidgets. Burns continues, "We simply could not function without his tireless efforts. So! A round of applause for: this inanimate carbon rod!" The carbon rod receives a commemorative medal while the crowd cheers (except Homer).

mood when talking to my coworker. . . . I came out of the back room to see if there was anything I could do. I noticed an error that my coworker and the client didn't notice and fixed the issue for them. The client was so impressed that he demanded to speak to my boss, and he told him how great I was. It was a very empowering feeling, and even though it was a small moment, I do believe that moment is when my boss really started noticing my hard work.

Notice the similarities here: The recognition is spontaneous— not part of a scheduled feedback session—and it is targeted at particular *behaviors.* A classic paper on recognition by Fred Luthans and Alexander D. Stajkovic emphasizes that effective recognition makes the employee feel *noticed* for what they've done. Managers are saying, "I saw what you did and I appreciate it."

Keith Risinger, who works in leadership development at Eli Lilly, has made recognition a hallmark of his management style. Earlier in his career, he managed a team of sales representatives who called on psychiatrists, hoping to convince them to adopt Lilly's drugs for use with their patients.

When Risinger visited his sales reps in the field, many of them would bring him to meet their best clients so they (the reps) would look like stars in front of the boss. But Bob Hughes was different. He asked for Risinger's help in handling one of his hardest customers, whom we'll call Dr. Singh. Hughes was frustrated by his lack of progress with Dr. Singh, who always seemed very interested in Lilly's drugs when Hughes was in the office, yet never prescribed the drugs they had discussed.

When Risinger shadowed Hughes on a visit to Dr. Singh's office, he noticed a big problem. Hughes was doing a great job *pitching* but he wasn't doing much listening. After the visit, Risinger asked Hughes some basic questions about the doctor: *How does he choose medications? How often does he see the patient he's treating? What measures for improvement does he trust?*

Hughes didn't have the answers. So Risinger challenged him to get more *curious* about his client—to stop giving a sales pitch and start learning what Dr. Singh thought. Over the next few visits, Hughes began to understand why Dr. Singh had been reluctant to change medications.

For example, one of Lilly's drugs, Zojcnz (disguised name), was designed for patients with ADHD (attention deficit/hyperactivity disorder). Dr. Singh saw a lot of ADHD patients, but he consistently prescribed other drugs over Zojenz. That puzzled Hughes, who thought Zojenz should be perfect for the doctor's patients: It was effective in treating ADHD, but unlike other medications, it wasn't a stimulant. Dr. Singh himself had praised the drug's profile. So why wasn't he providing it to his patients?

When Hughes started listening, he learned that many of Dr. Singh's ADHD patients were teenagers who came to him during a crisis—perhaps a student whose behavior problems had led him to the brink of a suspension or a failing grade. Patients in crisis needed help quickly. But Zojenz had a slow onset—unlike the stimulant drugs, it often required a month or more for its positive effects to kick in.

So Hughes suggested an option to Dr. Singh: Why not offer

Zojenz to your patients during the summer, when instant re-sults wouldn't be necessary? Hughes also suggested Zojenz for adult ADHD patients who might not be comfortable taking a stimulant.

Impressed, Dr. Singh began to try Zojenz with his patients and, liking the results he saw, he eventually became an advo-cate for it.

Risinger was thrilled by Hughes's work. This was exactly the kind of curiosity he wanted to instill in his reps.

About a month later, Risinger kicked off a sales meeting with the story of Hughes's progress with Dr. Singh, highlight-ing the value of asking more questions and *listening* to the an-swers. To commemorate the occasion he awarded Hughes a symbol of his quality listening: a pair of Bose headphones.

"That was a very proud moment for me," Hughes said. "People in the pharma industry are very intelligent and very competitive—to win that kind of award among your peers means more than being recognized with a bonus," he said.

Risinger began to use tailored rewards more often. To a rep who came up with a customized solution for an individual cli-ent, he gave a Keurig single-serve coffee machine (which lets you tailor each cup of coffee to the specific individual drinking it). To those who showed admirable curiosity about their cli-ents, he gave North Face gear that sported the tagline "Never stop exploring."

Pharmaceutical sales reps are well paid, and they can afford their own headphones and coffee machines. The prizes were symbols. With his half-silly gifts, Risinger created moments of pride for his team members.

Maybe your managerial style is different; maybe thematic gifts wouldn't work for you. There are many approaches to recognition. Some are spontaneous and no-nonsense: the manager above who complimented his employee for "cleaning and reorganizing all the bikes." Some are warm and caring: the teacher who took Kira Sloop's face in her hands and said, "You have a beautiful voice."

The style is not important. What's important is authenticity: being personal not programmatic. And frequency: closer to weekly than yearly. And of course what's most important is the message: "I saw what you did and I appreciate it."

4.

How do you deliver personal recognition when your scale forces it to be programmatic? Imagine a charity with thousands of donors. All of them deserve a thoughtful, personal reply—which is a logistical impossibility. But one charitable organization, DonorsChoose, has found a way to scale up thoughtfulness. Its leaders have methodically built a system to deliver recognition.

DonorsChoose's website allows teachers to seek crowd-sourced funding for school projects. An elementary school teacher might try to raise $250 to buy new books, or a high school science teacher might seek $600 to order new lab equipment. In an era of school budget cuts, this money from outside donors is precious.

For donors, the big moment comes a month or two later,

when most of them have forgotten their contributions. They receive a package in the mail full of individually written thank-you letters, addressed to them by name, from the students they supported.

Rabia Ahmad and her husband donated some money to buy basic supplies for an elementary school classroom. This was one of the letters they received:

Dear mr and ms Iman,

We thank you for our Pencels, folders, c dored Pencils, derase Markers, and our Papers we Preoheate it for all our Stuf I'm happy the class is happy my teacher und the school is very very happy I'm very very happ for our suplise I want to shout out to You thank You

Senserly,
Zion

"I cried," she said. "These kids—they're actually thanking me for giving them pencils."

Ahmad had been resistant to the idea of receiving thank-you letters. (The site's policy is that donors who give $50 or more will automatically receive thank-you notes, unless they opt out, which many do.) "This is something that no child should be thanking for," she thought. "We *expect* these supplies for our own children."

But after talking with the DonorsChoose staff, she realized that there were powerful benefits for the students, too: "It's not just getting the things, it's appreciating them. And realizing that there are people who want them to succeed."

Elementary school teacher Mary Jean Pace used Donors Choose to raise money for recycling bins for her school in Georgia. Many of her students' relatives chipped in, but the donation that clinched the project came from a woman in Arlington, Virginia. A stranger. Pace told her students, "Boys and girls, Arlington is a long way away and we don't even know her. And she thought what we are going to do is important." Her students were blown away. They couldn't wait to send notes to the woman in Arlington.

These thank-you letters have been part of the DonorsChoose experience since 2000, the year the organization was founded. In the beginning, the organization was sending hundreds of letters per year. In 2016, DonorsChoose distributed roughly a million! (See some recent samples on the next pages.)

This effort requires serious logistics, including a team of a dozen employees and 120 volunteers who help review letters. People frequently suggest that the operations could be made more efficient by scanning letters and distributing them via email. (Remember the warning earlier about the soul-sucking force of reasonableness.) "This act of facilitating gratitude goes against every recommendation about how to scale," said Julia Prieto, a vice president of DonorsChoose who oversees the donor letters. "But this is the one thing that people remember about their experience."

In 2014, the team analyzed historical data and discovered that donors who opt to receive thank-you letters will make larger donations the next year. The letters build commitment. But at DonorsChoose, the findings were almost beside the point.

"We're not in the marketing department," said Prieto. "We're not doing this to raise money. We believe it's an essential part of our model. We have consistently bet in the direction of gratitude." DonorsChoose has created a defining moments factory for donors.

Rabia Ahmad, the donor, reserves a special drawer in her desk for things she wants to hold on to, like her children's report cards. It's where she keeps the thank-you letters from DonorsChoose.

May 9, 2016

Dear Donor,
When I fell off my bike and hurt myself I had a lot of scabs, in fact, I still have some. The good thing was we used some scabs to look at under the microscope. They looked hairy and holy. I wonder why? More questions. I think that is what science is about.

Thank you for helping us by giving money to buy our microscope. It was very nice of you.

Sincerely,
Brandon

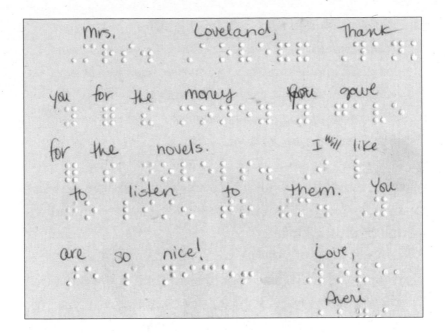

5.

Expressing gratitude pleases the *recipient* of the praise, of course, but it can also have a boomerang effect, elevating the spirits of the grateful person. Positive psychologists, who search for scientific ways to make people happier, have discovered the potency of what's called a "gratitude visit." Martin Seligman, the godfather of positive psychology, offers the following exercise:

> *Close your eyes. Call up the face of someone still alive who years ago did something or said something that changed your life for the better. Someone who you never properly thanked; someone you could meet face-to-face next week. Got a face?*

Your task is to write a letter of gratitude to this individual and deliver it in person. The letter should be concrete and about three hundred words: be specific about what she did for you and how it affected your life. Let her know what you are doing now, and mention how you often remember what she did.

As an example, consider this letter that University of Montana student Paul Glassman wrote to his mother and subsequently read aloud to her.

Mom, from when I was born to now, you have been impacting my life every day. . . .

When I was in high school, you came to every single sporting event that you possibly could, even if that meant you had to leave work early to catch the bus to get there. You were there. It didn't matter if I was playing down in Maple Valley during the playoffs, you were still there bundled in your blankets. Or if it was pouring rain in the middle of October, you were there in your raincoat. . . .

You pushed and pushed and pushed me to do well in school because you wanted me to go to college. I remember the day I was accepted to the University of Montana; we were both able to share that wonderful moment together. . . . I know that if it was not for you, I would not have continued my education, and I thank you for that. . . .

Through the toughest of times and through the best

of times, you have been there to support me, and I can't
honestly tell you what that means to me. All I can say
is that I love you with all of my heart. You are such
an amazing human being and an even better mother.
Thank you for all the time and effort and hard work you
have taken into making me the man that I am today. I
love you with all my heart.

It's clear why this visit would be a peak for Glassman's mother. It encompasses all four elements of a defining moment: ELEVATION, by breaking the script; INSIGHT, from hearing how her son views her; PRIDE in his accomplishments; and CONNECTION, sparked by the deep emotional message. (Both Glassman and his mother teared up during the reading of the letter.)

But the visit was also a defining moment for Glassman. In fact, he cited it as the third-most memorable experience of his college days, behind only graduation and attending the national championship game in football.

Researchers have found that if you conduct a gratitude visit, you feel a rush of happiness afterward—in fact, it's one of the most pronounced spikes that have been found in any positive psychology intervention. Glassman experienced it: "It was such an amazing feeling," he said. "I felt almost untouchable."

Better yet, researchers say, this feeling lasts. Even a month later, people who conducted a gratitude visit were still happier than their peers in a control group.

This is a stunning finding. There are a lot of pleasures in

the world that can spike our happiness for an hour—a warm doughnut comes to mind—but few that can still provide an afterglow a month later.

This disjunction—a small investment that yields a large reward—is the defining feature of recognition. A music teacher praises a troubled student's singing ability. A sales manager gives a pair of headphones as a prize. A boss spontaneously praises an employee for "prepping the backroom." All were moments of recognition that the recipients remembered and cherished for years afterward.

If you knew you could make a positive difference in someone's life—that you could create a memory for them that would last for years—and it would take only a trivial amount of time on your part, would you do it?

Well, now you know it.

Will you do it?

8

Multiply Milestones

1.

In 1996, when Josh Clark was 25, he had a bad breakup with his girlfriend, and it left him in a slump. So he started jogging. Clark hated jogging; he'd always hated jogging. But he thought this time might be different.

It wasn't. It was just as boring and painful as it had always been. But this time he stuck with it, and eventually he had "come out the other side," he said. The runs had started to feel different: meditative and relaxing. He could barely believe it. He never thought he was the kind of person who could enjoy running.

He felt "the zeal of the converted," he said, and he resolved to help other people discover the pleasures of jogging. Was there a way for someone to "get to the other side" without requiring the period of suffering he had endured? He wondered, *How do I give people easy victories?*

Clark started scribbling out a plan to ease people into running. People needed a goal, he thought. Something to look forward to. His hunch was that running in a 5K race would make a good goal—the races are public, social, competitive, and fun. (They are peaks.) And, critically, the 5K represented an attainable challenge, since most people in decent health could already *walk* a 5K.

So he called his plan "Couch to 5K." In 9 weeks, with 3 workouts per week, the plan would transform a couch-sitter into a 5K finisher. The first workout was simple: Alternating a 60-second jog with a 90-second walk for a total of 20 minutes. The workouts escalated steadily from there.

Clark needed a beta tester for his plan, so he called his mom. She was not receptive. "He was trying to convince me that I should get into this [running thing], too. Yeah, right," she said. But her maternal instincts kicked in, and she gave it a shot. It worked. She found it "kind of surprising that I could do it without a tremendous amount of effort or commitment."

Encouraged, Clark posted his plan to a website that he'd built for runners. It was 1997—the early days of the Web. "What surprised me was that people started picking it up and talking about it: 'I'm on week 3 day 2 and here's how it's going,'" Clark said.

Over the years, as interest in Couch to 5K grew, parts of the plan took on almost mythic qualities. For instance, in week 5 comes a moment that has spawned its own acronym: W5D3 (for week 5, day 3). This day requires the new joggers to step

up their efforts considerably. While the previous workout featured two 8-minute runs, separated by a walk, W5D3 requires a
continuous 20-minute jog, by far the longest stretch the participants have run to that point. It is feared and loathed by new joggers. In a blog post called "The Dreaded W5D3," one jogger
wrote, "I can think of at least 10 times where the old me would
have stopped to walk. Instead I shuffled along, sometimes very
slowly, until I regained my breath and was able to pick the pace
back up. I did it! . . . Woooooo!"

In 2000, Clark's website had picked up some advertisers,
and he decided to sell it to a company called Cool Runnings.
He went on with his life as an expert in software interface design, and meanwhile, over the years, his brainchild has grown
exponentially. Millions of people have heard of it (now known
as C25K), and hundreds of thousands have participated.

Clark has received countless emotional thank-yous from
people saying Couch to 5K changed their lives. He had meant
to introduce people to the joys of running, but in the process,
he had unwittingly delivered defining moments.

Billions of dollars have been spent trying to encourage
people to exercise. Most of it has been wasted. Yet here is a
program that has convinced thousands of people to train for a
3.1-mile jog. What gives?

The common goal to "get in shape" is ambiguous and un-
motivating. Pursuing it puts you on a path with no clear destination and no intermediate moments to celebrate. Couch to
5K provides a structure that respects the power of moments.
First, there's the commitment to join the program. That's one
milestone—it's a personal resolution made public. Surviving

the formidable W5D3 moment provides a second milestone. (The quote above says it all, "I did it! . . . Woooooo!" That's what pride sounds like.) And of course finishing the 5K is a peak, with elements of elevation and connection and pride. *Three months ago, I couldn't run 100 yards without heaving, and now I'm the kind of person who can finish a race!*

The C25K program *multiplies the milestones* that participants meet, and in so doing, it multiplies the pride that they experience. We can apply this same strategy to many aspects of our lives and work. To experience more defining moments, we need to rethink the way we set goals.

2.

Steve Kamb was a lifelong video game aficionado. An addict, even. He worried about how much of his life he was losing to the escapist pleasures of gaming. Then it occurred to him that he might be able to hijack his own addiction. If he could understand why he found games so compelling, he could use those same principles to rebuild his life "around adventure rather than escape."

In his book, *Level Up Your Life: How to Unlock Adventure and Happiness by Becoming the Hero of Your Own Story,* he described the structure of pleasurable games. They follow a system of levels: "When you are Level 1 and killing spiders, you know that when you kill enough spiders, you get to level up eventually and get to start attacking rats. Once you advance to a high enough level, you know you get to start slaying FREAK-ING DRAGONS (which can only be written in all caps)."

Conquering each level feels good. It feels so good, in fact, that you can love playing a game even if you never finish it. Think of it: Very few people finish Angry Birds or Candy Crush or (for that matter) Donkey Kong, but still they have a great time playing.

Kamb's insight was that, in our lives, we tend to declare goals without intervening levels. We declare that we're going to "learn to play the guitar." We take a lesson or two, buy a cheap guitar, futz around with simple chords for a few weeks. Then life gets busy, and seven years later, we find the guitar in the attic and think, *I should take up the guitar again.* There are no levels.

Kamb had always loved Irish music and had fantasized about learning to play the fiddle. So he co-opted gaming strategy and figured out a way to "level up" toward his goal:

LEVEL 1: Commit to one violin lesson per week, and practice 15 minutes per day for six months.

LEVEL 2: Relearn how to read sheet music and complete *Celtic Fiddle Tunes* by Craig Duncan.

LEVEL 3: Learn to play "Concerning Hobbits" from *The Fellowship of the Ring* on the violin.

LEVEL 4: Sit and play the fiddle for 30 minutes with other musicians.

LEVEL 5: Learn to play "Promontory" from *The Last of the Mohicans* on the violin.

BOSS BATTLE: Sit and play the fiddle for 30 minutes in a pub in Ireland.

Isn't that ingenious? He's taken an ambiguous goal—learning to play the fiddle—and defined an appealing destination: playing in an Irish pub. Better yet, he invented five milestones en route to the destination, each worthy of celebration. Note that, as with a game, if he stopped the quest after Level 3, he'd still have several moments of pride to remember. It would have been a fun ride, like quitting after 30 levels of Candy Crush.

Could you adapt this strategy for one of your goals? Many Americans aspire to learn another language, for example. But "learning Spanish" is one of those amorphous goals that should give us pause. There's no destination and no intermediate levels. Using Kamb's principles, we can make this a more exciting journey. We can *level up*:

LEVEL 1: Order a meal in Spanish.

LEVEL 2: Have a simple conversation in Spanish with a taxi driver.

LEVEL 3: Glance at a Spanish newspaper and understand at least one headline.

LEVEL 4: Follow the action in a Spanish cartoon.

LEVEL 5: Read a kindergarten-level book in Spanish.

And so on, leading up to . . .

DESTINATION: Be able to have full, normal conversations in Spanish with Fernando in accounting (not just "Cómo está usted?")

Compare that plan with the typical way we think about pursuing goals:

LEVEL 1: Try to squeeze in a Spanish study session.

LEVEL 2: Try to squeeze in a Spanish study session.

LEVEL 3: Try to squeeze in a Spanish study session.

LEVEL 4: Try to squeeze in a Spanish study session.

LEVEL 5: Try to squeeze in a Spanish study session.

DESTINATION: Someday, eventually: "Know" Spanish.

Which of those plans sound like more fun? Which are you more likely to return to, if you're forced to take a break? Which are you more likely to complete?

3.

By using Kamb's level-up strategy, we multiply the number of motivating milestones we encounter en route to a goal. That's a forward-looking strategy: We're anticipating moments of pride ahead. But the opposite is also possible: to *surface* those milestones you've already met but might not have noticed. Earlier in the book, we mentioned the way Fitbit celebrates its customers for fitness milestones: The India badge, for instance, celebrates you for walking a total of 1,997 miles, which is the length of India. (Celebrating 2,000 miles walked would have been fitting, too, but somehow the India badge feels more interesting and memorable.) No Fitbit customers would have been aware of this feat had the company not told them.

But this instinct to notice and commemorate achievements is oddly lacking in many areas of life. Take youth sports leagues. There are natural moments of pride scattered throughout the season: points scored, victories won. But what about the kids' *greater skill at basketball*?

Certainly the kids know, in a generic sense, that they've improved over the course of a season. But improvements are slow and incremental. Almost invisible. You can't rewind your memory to six months prior and observe how clearly your dribbling has improved.

But you can rewind a *video*. What if every boy on a basketball team received a simple before-and-after video comparing his performance at the beginning and end of the season? The improvements would be so obvious, so visible: *Check it out—I could barely dribble with my left hand! Haha—I couldn't make a free throw to save my life*. What a stunning moment of pride that would be. *Look how far I've come!* And yet we have not encountered a single coach who has had the instinct to mint this moment of pride for his players.

Or think about how couples celebrate their anniversaries: by taking trips, going out for a nice dinner, or exchanging gifts. Those are moments rich with elevation and connection. But what about pride? Shouldn't couples acknowledge and celebrate what they've accomplished together?

One couple we know kept an anniversary journal for the first decade of their marriage. Every year they would record the things they accomplished: Redecorating the back bedroom, hosting extended family for Thanksgiving dinner, and so on. They'd also record the trips they took, and the friends they saw most frequently, and, amazingly, what they fought about!

The husband said, "Reliving the big arguments from the previous year is not for the faint of heart, because you tend to want to refight them." But having the record was useful because it provided concrete evidence of the progress they had made in their relationship. In the first year of marriage, they fought about almost anything. (One actual example: Which spices can stay on the kitchen table?) Over the next three years, the arguments steadily dwindled, and by the fifth year, they could recall only minor bickering. Not even an honest-to-goodness fight. And they laughed at the memory of fighting over spices.

That's a laugh that signals a moment of pride. *Look at how far we've come.* And that moment would not have happened, we suspect, were it not for the journal.

4.

What's clear from the preceding is that we are consistently missing opportunities to create moments of pride for ourselves and others. The interesting question is, *Why?*

Our theory: We've been brainwashed by the goals we see in our work lives. Executives tend to set goals that sound like this: Grow revenues to $20 billion by 2020! (That's a real example, by the way. Based on our experience with C-suite executives, we think it's likely that millions of people around the world are working, at this very moment, toward goals that were chosen simply because the numbers had a catchy ring.)

Similar goals cascade downward. Within the organization with the "$20B by 2020" goal, a particular business unit might have a smaller supporting goal: *Increase market share in South America to 23% by 2018.* Then, after setting a goal like that, the group would make a bunch of plans to achieve it.

A numerical goal plus supporting plans. Notice what that combination leaves us with: A destination that is not inherently motivating and that lacks meaningful milestones along the way. As a result, achieving the "20 by 2020" goal will require a massive human effort with much of the pride stripped out.

To be fair, this combination of goal-setting and planning can move an organization in the right direction. But the value of these tools comes from holding people accountable for their work. They're not designed to be intrinsically motivating or to improve the experience of the human beings who are being held accountable.

We should be careful that we don't let this corporate style of goal-setting infiltrate our personal lives, where we're in full control. "I'm going to lose 10 pounds in 2 months," for instance, is a classic corporate goal: arbitrary, numerical, and lacking intermediate milestones. By now, you know what to do: Restore the milestones. Level up: *Go one week straight without using the elevator. Pick out 2 microbrews to enjoy on Saturday after a full week without booze. If I jog continuously for three songs on my playlist, that entitles me to download three new ones.* And so on.

Furthermore, the ultimate destination should not be "losing 10 pounds," it should be something intrinsically motivating, such as "Fitting into my sexy black pants (without gastrointestinal distress)." Suddenly, your weight-loss mission starts looking more like a playful quest, with frequent victories along the way, and less like a daily weigh-in on the bathroom scale

Is there a way to channel this same spirit *inside* organizations—to counteract the "command and control" culture of goals and plans? A wise leader can look for milestones en route to a larger goal. Let's say your group has been tasked with boosting customer satisfaction by 20% by the end of the third quarter. You might have no control over that goal and how it's framed. But you can still multiply the milestones for your team (note that these need not be sequential):

> **MILESTONE 1:** Receive a glowing thank-you from a well-satisfied customer.
>
> **MILESTONE 2:** Make it a full week without any surveys scoring their satisfaction as a 1 out of 7.
>
> **MILESTONE 3:** Solve the number one complaint from the last month of surveys.
>
> **MILESTONE 4:** Get halfway there: Boost satisfaction by 10%.
>
> And so on . . .

To identify milestones like these, ask yourself: What's *inherently* motivating? (Getting a glowing thank-you.) What would be worth celebrating that might only take a few weeks or months of work? (Solving the number one complaint.) What's a hidden accomplishment that is worth *surfacing and celebrating*? (Making it a full week without any 1s.)

The same logic applies to milestones involving less tangible goals, such as building leadership skills. In most organizations, the only clear "levels" en route to leadership positions are promotions. But what if it takes five years for an employee to earn a promotion, or what if she is not interested in or suited for a promotion? How do you create the intermediate milestones that could provide moments of pride?

Large organizations often speak in terms of "competencies." That is, to do a particular job well, you need to develop a set of specific competencies in areas such as *vision setting* or *business acumen* or *data analysis*. (Yes, they tend to sound exactly that boring.)

But rather than giving vague instructions to employees on how to build their "business acumen," they could be presented instead with a set of meaningful milestones to accomplish (again, not necessarily sequential):

- Turn around a product/service line that is struggling
- Have a direct report promoted to a managerial role
- Solve a business challenge by collaborating with another function or group
- Receive a compliment that you run meetings that are actually worthwhile
- Deliver a major project on time and on budget
- Contribute an idea that is adopted company-wide

These items would not be a checklist for advancement (*Do these 6 things and you'll be promoted*), since it would be impossible to create a generic list that would apply to all people and situations. Rather, the milestones would simply map out the turf of achievement. *Here are the ways it's possible to build your skills and demonstrate your value to the organization. And when you do so, we will salute you for that.*

5.

Hitting a milestone sparks pride. It should also spark a celebration—a moment of elevation. (Don't forget that milestones, along with pits and transitions, are three natural defining moments that deserve extra attention.) Milestones deserve peaks.

The Boy Scouts understand this idea well. The Scouts' Merit Badge program, active for more than 100 years, is a great example of introducing multiple milestones and celebrating each one. The Merit Badges are presented to the Scout at a "Court of Honor," where the Scouts are recognized in front of their peers. That's a peak. Similarly, karate students who earn belts—from the novice's white belt to the expert's black belt—often receive them at public award ceremonies.

People who develop lifelong passions are often honoring these same concepts, whether consciously or not. In 2013, Scott Ettl, an executive at a research firm and the father of three young kids, read a book about Aaron Burr that a friend had recommended. Burr, the third vice president of the United States and the man who famously killed Alexander Hamilton in a duel, was portrayed as an American hero. Then, a few weeks later, Ettl devoured David McCullough's bestselling biography of John Adams, which cast Burr in a negative light.

He read a biography of George Washington and, sure enough, it portrayed John Adams differently than had Mc-Cullough's biography. But by the time he had read about the same people and events for the third time (since Washington, Adams, and Burr all overlapped), his perception of history, as he had learned it in school, began to change. The portraits of the historical figures stopped feeling flat and contradictory; rather, they began to acquire three dimensions.

He was hooked. He'd always been a history buff, but the biographies were bringing a kind of order to his passion. One day, he made a declaration to his family: He was going to read a biography of every American president, in order. "It became more than liking history," he said. "It became a quest." A quest with 45 ready-made milestones.

He blazed through the first 8 or 9 presidential biographies in the first year. The Millard Fillmore book slowed him down, and then his quest was almost derailed by the Rutherford B. Hayes biography—"about the worst book you could possibly imagine," he said. It took him a year to finish it.

The quest has evolved over time. Now when Ettl completes a president, he buys the commemorative dollar coin for that president from the U.S. Mint. The coins provide a visual token of his progress, as do the presidential autographs his relatives started to buy for him.

Remember in the first chapter, we talked about the "treasure chest" of items that we all keep for ourselves, full of old awards and ticket stubs and journals? Ettl's treasure chest is full of hardcover books, historic coins, and aged autographs—the relics of his march through U.S. history. There's something appealing about a moment of pride that comes with its own souvenir.

Think about how good it feels to flip through the stamps on your passport. A mere smudge of ink can provoke a rush of memories. (In keeping with this spirit, shouldn't boarding passes be designed to be "treasure chest" items? When you visit San Francisco, your stub should have the Golden Gate Bridge on it. Instead, we're given boarding documents that look like the homework of a dot-matrix printer.)

Ettl estimates it will take him about 2–3 years to catch up to the current president. "Unless I die, I'll finish this," he vowed.

When he catches up to the present-day president, Ettl said, he plans to start taking his family on vacations to the presidential libraries. In other words, the end of one quest will be the start of another! (Though we wonder whether this idea has been run by the kids.)

6.

Look at the graph below, which comes from researcher George Wu at the University of Chicago. It summarizes the completion times of more than nine million runners in marathons from Chicago to Berlin. You can see that most runners finished a marathon in 3.5 to 5 hours.

But notice how the graph looks spiky. Pay attention to the vertical lines showing the "threshold" times: 4:00:00, 4:30:00, 5:00:00, and so forth. You'll see that a lot more runners finished just before the lines than just after them. (It's particularly dramatic at the 4-hour mark.)

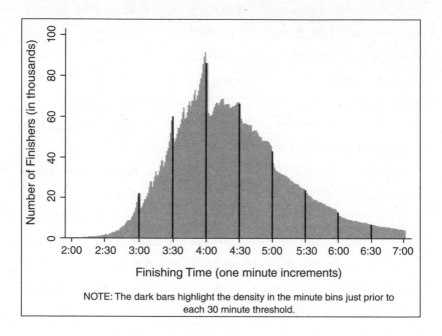

NOTE: The dark bars highlight the density in the minute bins just prior to each 30 minute threshold.

That's the milestone effect. That's an exhausted runner who turns on her afterburners with one mile to go because she cannot bear to let the numbers on the stopwatch cross 4 hours. The milestones are completely arbitrary, of course: There is no defensible performance difference between 3:59:59 and 4:00:00. But of course, you understand the difference, and so do we. (One of your authors will sometimes walk laps around his bedroom at night in order to clinch 10,000 steps for the day. Absurd but true.)

We all love milestones.

This brings us to one last point: The desire to hit milestones elicits a concerted final push of effort. To finish the marathon under 4 hours, you sprint the final quarter mile. To hit your 10,000 steps for the day, you obsessively pace the bedroom.

Cal Newport, an author and computer science professor, spent years studying the habits of successful people. "From my experience, the most common trait you will consistently observe in accomplished people is an obsession with completion. Once a project falls into their horizon, they crave almost compulsively, to finish it."

Success comes from pushing to the finish line. What milestones do is *compel us* to make that push, because (a) they're within our grasp, and (b) we've chosen them precisely because they're worth reaching for. Milestones define moments that are conquerable and worth conquering.

A Boy Scout spends one more day practicing with his bow and arrow, so he can nail the test and earn his archery badge. Scott Ettl suffers through Millard Fillmore's biography because he knows Lincoln's is coming. They push to the finish line.

But here's the best part: We're not stuck with just one finish line. By multiplying milestones, we transform a long, amorphous race into one with many intermediate "finish lines." As we push through each one, we experience a burst of pride as well as a jolt of energy to charge toward the next one.

9

Practice Courage

1.

On February 13, 1960, a group of black students led by John Lewis, Angela Butler, and Diane Nash filed into several stores in downtown Nashville and took seats at the whites-only lunch counters. It was the start of Nashville's first sit-in to protest segregation.

"The students were dressed like they were on the way to church," said John Lewis, now a longtime congressman from Georgia, in an interview featured in *Eyes on the Prize*, the excellent PBS series on the civil rights movement, from which this account was drawn. "We stayed there at the lunch counter studying and preparing our homework because we were denied service. The manager ordered that the lunch counters be closed, that the restaurants be closed."

"The first sit-in we had was really funny because the waitresses were nervous and they must have dropped $2,000 worth of dishes that day," said Diane Nash. "I mean, literally it was almost a cartoon . . . she was so nervous, she picked up dishes and she dropped one and she'd pick up another one and she'd drop it."

The students were uniformly peaceful and polite, and the sit-in concluded without incident, as did the second sit-in the following week. But at the third sit-in, on February 27, the threat escalated. The students were harassed and heckled by young whites who had gathered in the stores. Several of the demonstrators were pulled from their seats and assaulted. When the police arrived to respond to the violence, 77 black students were arrested for loitering and disorderly conduct. None of the hostile whites were arrested.

The students were convicted of disorderly conduct. John Lewis, among other students, refused to pay the $50 fine and chose instead to spend a month in jail.

Meanwhile, the parents of the students, horrified that their children had been jailed, rallied the black community around a new idea: a boycott of the segregated downtown stores. "Let's stop supporting the system we're trying to change," said student activist Leo Lillard. "We figured if [the store owners] would feel the pinch of not having shoppers buy in the stores in downtown Nashville, then that will put pressure on the mayor, on the political fabric of town, of Nashville, to change the rules, the regulations."

Then, in the early morning of April 19, a bomb was thrown into the home of Z. Alexander Looby, the lawyer for the black students. The blast was devastating—powerful enough to shatter 147 windows in a college dormitory across the street. Miraculously, Looby and his wife, sleeping in a back bedroom, were unhurt.

The assassination attempt outraged the community. Black leaders organized a march to City Hall. "People began to gather, and we began to march and students came out from the lunchrooms and they came out from being on the campus grounds," said Rev. C. T. Vivian. "We filled Jefferson Avenue . . . we walked by a place where there were workers out for the noon hour, white workers and they had never seen anything like this. And here was all the 4,000 people marching down the street, and all you could hear was their feet as we silently moved. And [the white workers] didn't know what to do and they moved back up against the wall and they simply stood against the wall, just looking. There was a fear there, there was an awe, and they did not know what to do. But they knew that this was not to be stopped, this was not to be played with or to be joked with."

On the steps of City Hall, Rev. Vivian and Diane Nash confronted the mayor, Ben West, in front of the large and growing crowd. Nash said, "Mayor West, do you feel that it's wrong to discriminate against a person solely on the basis of his race or color?" West agreed it was wrong.

Then, Nash continued, shouldn't lunch counters be desegregated?

"Yes," Mayor West admitted.

Many in the white community were inflamed by the mayor's response. Nevertheless, three weeks later, the lunch counters reversed their discriminatory policies, and for the first time, black customers were served alongside whites. The desegregation of the lunch counters in Nashville was one of the first big successes of the civil rights movement.

It was a victory built on courage—the courage of a group of students who were willing to face humiliation, injury, and incarceration to protest immoral treatment. For the students involved, taking a seat at those lunch counters was a defining moment in their lives. And their efforts grew into a defining moment for the nation.

What's less well known about this story is that the demonstrators didn't just *show* courage. They *practiced* it. They *rehearsed* it. And this brings us to the story of a remarkable figure in the civil rights movement: James Lawson.

Lawson, a Methodist minister, had traveled to India to learn the techniques of nonviolent resistance from the disciples of Mahatma Gandhi. When he moved to Nashville, he began to train many of the people who would become leaders in the civil rights movement: Lewis, Nash, and others. Lawson believed strongly in preparation for resistance: "You cannot go on a demonstration with 25 people doing whatever they want to do. They have to have a common discipline; that's a key word for me. The difficulty with nonviolent people and efforts is that they don't recognize the necessity of fierce discipline and training."

In Nashville, Lawson held workshops to train protesters. "He told the crowd how to behave in the face of a hundred possible emergencies, how to avoid violating the loitering laws, how to move to and from the lunch counters in orderly shifts, how to fill the seats of students who needed to go to the bathroom, even how to dress: stockings and heels for the women, coats and ties for the fellows," wrote the historian Taylor Branch.

But Lawson didn't just offer advice; he insisted that students engage in role-plays. He mocked up a lunch counter, based on the real ones in the downtown stores, and asked students to take their place on the stools. Then, white men—confederates of Lawson—encroached on the students' space, crowding them. The men shouted racial slurs at the students. They'd lean in, inches from the students' faces, and insult them. A few of the men flicked cigarette ashes into the students' hair. They shoved students off the stools, onto the floor, manhandling them and pulling at their clothes.

The simulated attacks were brutal but essential. Lawson wanted to inoculate the students with the instinct of resistance—the ability to suppress the natural urges to fight back or run away. By the time John Lewis and his peers took their places at the real lunch counters in downtown Nashville, they were ready. Disciplined, polite, unflappable. They were afraid, of course, but they had learned to restrain their fear. As Mark Twain said, "Courage is resistance to fear, mastery of fear—not absence of fear."

2.

When people recount the proudest moments of their lives, they tend to start with their loved ones. *The day I got married.*

The day my child was born. The day my child graduated from college. These are natural defining moments.

Then people tend to share proud moments of achievement: barriers overcome, victories won, successes earned. In the past two chapters, we've studied ways to create more of these moments: first, by recognizing the accomplishments of others, and second, by multiplying the milestones that we conquer en route to our goals.

So we take pride in the people we love, and we take pride in our own achievements. But there's something missing here. Consider how people describe other moments of pride: *I stood up for someone. I held firm and took the heat. I made a stand that I believed in. I refused to cave.* These sentiments don't describe "achievements," at least in the sense of plaques and certificates. Rather, they are describing moments of courage.

Moments of courage may seem harder to "create" than the others we've encountered in this section. After all, we can *choose* when we recognize someone; we can *choose* when and how to multiply milestones. But moments that demand courage often arrive unexpectedly. They're fleeting, and we can be caught off guard. Too often the moment passes and we find ourselves wishing later that we'd spoken up or done something.

You can't manufacture "moments of courage." But in this chapter we'll see that you can *practice* courage so that, when the moment demands it, you'll be ready.

The military understands this concept well. As the psychologist S. J. Rachman wrote in a report on military training,

"What might be called 'training for courage' plays an important part in preparing people to undertake dangerous jobs such as fire-fighting or parachuting."

Rachman studied soldiers who were responsible for disabling improvised explosive devices (IEDs) during the conflict in Northern Ireland. It's dangerous work, of course. From 1969 to 1981, more than 31,000 incidents were dealt with, and 17 bomb-disposal operators were killed in action.

Rachman wrote that the "successful practice of courageous performance" led to a reduction in fear and a bolstering of confidence. Novice bomb-disposal operators were put through a regimen of training that simulated the situations they'd experience in the field. The effect on the operators' confidence was striking: After completing the simulations, they expressed 80% of the confidence reported by experienced operators. That's a remarkable level of confidence for people who had not yet de-activated a bomb in the field! (Nor did their confidence seem to reflect naïve optimism: Their estimates of the *danger* of the work were similar to those of experienced operators.)

What made the training so effective? "One element of such training, the gradual and graduated practice of the dangerous tasks likely to be encountered, seems to be especially valuable," Rachman said.

That element—"gradual and graduated practice"—is also the hallmark of *exposure therapy*, one of the most effective techniques for reducing phobias (irrational fears). In a study led by Jayson Mystkowski, the researchers applied exposure therapy to people terrified of spiders. At the beginning of the study, the participants were asked to get as close as they could tolerate to a tarantula contained in a terrarium. The average participant stopped 10 feet away.

Over the course of the experiment, they were asked to practice courage in 14 graduated steps. Each step was first demonstrated by the researcher; then, the participants were asked to repeat the task when they felt ready. Here's a sampling:

STEP 1: Stand 5 feet from the tarantula inside its terrarium.

STEP 3: Place the palm of your hand against the closed container near the tarantula.

STEP 7: Direct the tarantula's movement with a small paintbrush 5 times.

STEP 9: Let the tarantula walk over a heavily gloved hand.

Notice that this is basically a level-up plan, where each step constitutes a concrete and prideworthy moment. ("You won't believe this, but I TOUCHED A TARANTULA today. Granted, it was with a paintbrush, but still, it counts!")

The long series of steps culminated with Step 14: allowing the tarantula to walk on the participant's *uncovered* hand. Take a guess: How long do you think it took these arachnophobes to reach Step 14? That is, to reach the point where they would voluntarily allow a big hairy tarantula to take a leisurely stroll across their palm? Weeks? Months?

Try two hours. That was the average time to complete Step 14, and astonishingly, *all* the participants succeeded. These were people who couldn't get within 10 feet of the terrarium a short while earlier! Even more impressive, six months later, they could still touch the spider.

"Before treatment, some of these participants wouldn't walk on grass for fear of spiders or would stay out of their home or dorm room for days if they thought a spider was present," said lead author Katherina Hauner.

We often replicate "exposure therapy" in our own lives. Think of a parent trying to coax a nervous child to relax around a friendly dog. *Look at what that beagle is doing, he's so silly . . . Do you want to see him chew his toy? . . . He's sitting down now—do you want to pat his furry back? . . . He loves treats—do you want to give him one?* And soon your child has a new best friend.

Managing fear—the goal of exposure therapy—is a critical part of courage. The civil rights demonstrator and the bomb-disposal operator must be able to control their fears to be successful. But courage isn't just suppressed fear. It's also the knowledge of how to act in the moment.

Recall that James Lawson had given students direction on "how to avoid violating the loitering laws, how to move to and from the lunch counters in orderly shifts, how to fill the seats of students who needed to go to the bathroom," and so on. His workshops weren't just about toughening up emotionally. They were about mental rehearsals. Participants had to anticipate how they would react to certain situations. In a sense, they were preloading a response so that, in the moment, they could act quickly without deliberation.

The psychologist Peter Gollwitzer has studied the way this preloading affects our behavior. His research shows that when people make advance mental commitments—if X happens, then I will do Y—they are substantially more likely to act in support of their goals than people who lack those mental plans. Someone who has committed to drink less alcohol, for instance, might resolve, "Whenever a waiter asks if I want a second drink, I'll ask for sparkling water." And that person is far more likely to turn down the drink than someone else who *shares the same goal* but has no preloaded plan.

Gollwitzer calls these plans "implementation intentions," and often the trigger for the plan is as simple as a time and place: *When I leave work today, I'm going to drive straight to the gym.* The success rate is striking. Setting implementation intentions more than doubled the number of students who turned in a certain assignment on time; doubled the number of women who performed breast self-exams in a certain month; and cut by half the recovery time required by patients who had received hip or knee replacement (among many other examples). There is power in preloading a response.

This preloading is what's often missing in organizational situations that require courage. A colleague or client belittles someone, or makes an off-color remark, or suggests something unethical, and we're so taken aback that we do nothing. Ten minutes later, we curse ourselves for not acting. We missed our chance.

These missed opportunities made Mary Gentile reconsider the way we teach ethics in schools. Gentile, a a professor at the University of Virginia Darden School of Business, realized that ethics education was dominated by the question, "What is the right thing to do?" But people often know what the right thing to do is. The hard part is acting on that judgment.

"We can all generate a list of what makes this hard to do," Gentile said. "We feel alone; we wonder if we're being naïve; we wonder if we're misinformed (or we want to believe that perhaps we are); we wonder if our boss will be receptive; we anticipate that we will encounter 'push back' if we raise the issue and we don't know what we'll say when that happens; we worry about being ostracized or worse if we appear not to be a 'team player.'"

She became convinced that ethics education should focus not on WHAT *is the right thing to do?* but rather on HOW *can I get the right thing done?* She created a curriculum called Giving Voice to Values, which has been used in more than 1,000 schools and organizations.

The heart of her strategy is practice. You identify situations where an ethical issue might arise. You anticipate the rationalizations you'll hear for the behavior. Then you literally script out your possible response or action. And finally you practice that response with peers.

Leaders who want to instill an ethical business culture — and not just mouth the words of a toothless "statement of values" — will take inspiration from Gentile and make practice a priority. Because the situations that lead to unethical behavior are predictable: A relentless pressure for results, coupled with avert-the-eyes management, will lead to cut corners or outright fraud (think banking scandals). Blurry lines of accountability, plus get-things-done urgency, will lead to accidents (think cataclysmic oil spills). A leader's bias or bigotry or sexism, taking root in a permissive environment, will inevitably lead to abuse.

These are not anomalies. They are probabilities. They can be foreseen and fought.

"Just as an athlete practices his or her moves to commit them to muscle memory, the point here is to make voicing our values the default position," said Gentile.

3.

At the seminary at Yeshiva University, students role-played difficult situations with actors, modeling the crises they might face as a rabbi dealing with congregants. As reported by Paul Vitello in the *New York Times*, the situations they rehearsed are complex and emotional: Talking with a suicidal teenager. Comforting an elderly woman frustrated with the indignities and invisibility of old age. Counseling a victim of childhood sexual abuse. Telling a man his wife had died of an aneurysm while visiting the synagogue.

That last scenario was presented to the 24-year-old student Benjamin Houben. Here's how Vitello describes the scene: "To prepare for the scene, [Houben] paused outside the room, trying to conjure the feeling of death. He entered the classroom, wearing a look of grief that he hoped would telegraph what he was about to say. But the actor was not about to make the job easier. He waited to be told, then he went to pieces with 'great skill,' said Mr. Houben, whose face seemed to sag just retelling the scene. . . . The lessons he learned from the simulation, he said, were these: People may not believe you when you tell them. It may take a long time for them to absorb the shock. And after that, it only gets worse."

Originally in the role-playing exercises there were no actors—the students role-played with each other. But there was a problem. "It wasn't real enough," said Rabbi Menachem Penner, the dean of the seminary. "It was instructional but not experiential. It was the difference between reading something in a book and living through it. The actors created the level of tension that really made it valuable."

A crucial feature of practicing courage, then, is making sure the practice requires courage! In the Nashville rehearsals, James Lawson's confederates cursed at the student protesters. Mocked them. Shoved them. And Rabbi Penner's seminary students must confront congregants who scream and cry and break down. In the back of their minds, the students know it's not "real," but the moment feels real.

The students gain confidence from rehearsing such fraught and delicate conversations. "We've found that when students practice, even for one session, it makes them so much calmer and more prepared when they have to do it in real life," said Rabbi Penner. It takes courage to offer counsel in such traumatic situations, and that courage is strengthened with practice.

In most organizations, employees won't be called on to deal with situations this grave, but at some point everyone will face an anxiety-making conversation. How do you stand up to a dictatorial boss? How do you say "no" to an important customer? How do you fire an employee who might lash out? How do you lay off a loyal employee whose role is no longer needed? Every industry has its own unique set of emotional encounters: An airline desk agent who must help an irate passenger who's missed his connecting flight by 90 seconds. A teacher who must tell a student's parents that their child is behaving badly. A financial advisor who must inform an elderly widow she's lost a fifth of her nest egg because of a stock market correction.

Practice quiets the anxiety that can cloud our mind in a tough moment. When we lack practice, our good intentions often falter. As an example, take the antidrug program D.A.R.E. (Drug Abuse Resistance Education), launched in 1983, which invites police officers into schools to inform students about the harms of drugs and to encourage a drug-free lifestyle. It's an admirable and well-intentioned intervention, and it's popular. It's the most widely used drug prevention program in the United States. But the evidence from several studies is clear: It doesn't work. One meta-analysis found that teens enrolled in D.A.R.E. were just as likely to use drugs as those who weren't.

Why doesn't D.A.R.E. work? Clues about the program's flaws can be found in the work of Pim Cuijpers, who studied what made antidrug programs successful. Cuijpers's research had led to a simple conclusion: Programs that reduce drug use employ *interactive* methods, while ineffective programs don't.

In other words, to resist drugs, students need the opportunity to practice courage. The hard part isn't knowing what the right thing to do is. The hard part is doing it. There will come a time at a party when a 16-year-old is offered alcohol or marijuana. If they haven't rehearsed what they'll do or say in that moment, they are likely to feel their resolve crumble.

What teens may not realize is that if they resist drugs or alcohol, they will make it easier for others to resist, too. An act of courage can bolster the resolve of others. One executive gave us an example of how he acts on this insight in his business. "When we have meetings, I typically have a 'plant' in the audience and give them a tough question to ask," he said. "It's always a question we know people are asking and talking about but afraid to actually bring to leadership. I do this to 'pop the cork' and show that it's safe." He's right to be concerned about people staying silent: One study found that 85% of workers felt "unable to raise an issue or concern to their bosses even though they felt the issue was important."

His solution—the confederate with the tough question—is well supported by evidence. There's a classic study, conducted by Charlan Nemeth and Cynthia Chiles, demonstrating that one act of courage supports another. Let's say you are a participant in the study. You are matched with three other people, and a researcher shows your group a series of 20 slides. After each one is presented, the researcher pauses to ask each of you what color the slide is. It's an easy task: All the slides are blue, and all four of you say "blue" all 20 times you're asked.

Then, that group breaks up and you are put into a new group of four. Same task. This time, though, the first slide is red. Oddly, all three of your group-mates call it "orange." What will you call it? It certainly looks red, but could you be wrong? This happens 19 more times—your group-mates always call the slides "orange" and, each time, everyone looks at you to hear your answer.

If you think you would stay strong in this situation, you might be right, but you'd be in the minority. Most people in the study caved. On average, they called 14 of the 20 red slides "orange," conforming to the majority's incorrect view. (The three people in the group who claimed all the red slides were "orange" were, as you might have guessed, confederates of the researchers.)

Another set of participants were ushered through the sequence above but with one crucial difference: This time, the researchers also added a confederate to the first group (the one viewing blue slides). He was instructed to call all the blue sides "green." Let's call him the Brave but Wrong Guy. The other three (normal) participants were probably puzzled by his seeming color-blindness, but they easily stuck to their guns, calling all the blue slides "blue."

The striking change came in the second group. The participants were shown the red slides, and as described above, the three confederates continually called them "orange." This time, though, the participants stayed strong! They defied the majority, labeling 17 out of 20 slides (on average) as red.

Note that they were brave even though they hadn't practiced courage themselves. They'd only *witnessed* it. Brave but Wrong Guy was willing to speak up for himself—even though he was mistaken about the color. That act of dissent bolstered the other participants' resolve. As the researchers wrote, "exposure to a dissenting minority view, even when that view is in error, contributes to independence."

The bad news here is that our natural instinct is to cave to the majority opinion. If everyone says the red card is orange, we think we must be wrong, and we call it orange, too.

The good news is that if even one person is brave enough to defy the majority, we are emboldened. We're not alone anymore. We're not crazy. And we feel we can call red "red."

In short, courage is contagious. From historic protests to everyday acts, from the civil rights movement to an employee asking a tough question, this is the lesson we've learned: It is hard to be courageous, but it's easier when you've practiced, and when you stand up, others will join you.

Think of it: Your moment of courage might be a defining moment for someone else—a signal to them that red is red, that wrong is wrong, and that it can be righted if we stand, together, against it.

MOMENTS OF PRIDE
THE WHIRLWIND REVIEW

1. Moments of pride commemorate people's achievements. We feel our chest puff out and our chin lift.

2. There are three practical principles we can use to create more moments of pride: (1) Recognize others; (2) Multiply meaningful milestones; (3) Practice courage. The first principle creates defining moments for others; the latter two allow us to create defining moments for ourselves.

3. We dramatically underinvest in recognition.
   - *Researcher Wiley: 80% of supervisors say they frequently express appreciation, while less than 20% of employees agree.*

4. Effective recognition is personal, not programmatic. ("Employee of the Month" doesn't cut it.)
   - *Risinger at Eli Lilly used "tailored rewards" (e.g., Bose headphones) to show his team: I saw what you did and I appreciate it.*

5. Recognition is characterized by a disjunction: A small investment of effort yields a huge reward for the recipient.
   - *Kira Sloop, the middle school student, had her life changed by a music teacher who told her that her voice was beautiful.*

6. To create moments of pride for ourselves, we should multiply meaningful milestones—reframing a long journey so that it features many "finish lines."
   - *The author Kamb planned ways to "level up"—for instance "Learn how to play 'Concerning Hobbits' from* The Fellowship of the Ring*"—toward his long-term goal of mastering the fiddle.*

7. We can also surface milestones that would have gone unnoticed.

- *What if every member of a youth sports team got a "before-and-after" video of their progress?*
- *Number-heavy organizational goals are fine as tools of accountability, but smart leaders surface more motivational milestones en route to the target.*

8. Moments when we display courage make us proud. We never know when courage will be demanded, but we can practice to ensure we're ready.
   - *The protesters involved in the Nashville lunch counter sit-ins didn't just show courage, they rehearsed it.*

9. Practicing courage lets us "preload" our responses.
   - *Gentile's approach to ethics says we usually know WHAT is right but don't know HOW to act.*

10. Courage is contagious; our moments of action can be a defining moment for others.

—————— **Clinic 4** ——————
Boss Has Flash of Insight: I'm a Jerk

The situation: The CFO of a company—let's call him Mark—has just reviewed the results of his 360 feedback. The results are not good.

Mark knows that he is not well loved in the company. He prides himself on being a tell-it-like-it-is manager. "Leadership is not a popularity contest," he'll say. Even so, he is shocked by the feedback. People don't see him as a no-nonsense leader. They see him as a total jerk. He rarely listens, they said. He interrupts people frequently to insert his own views. He is dismissive of other people's opinions. And he never apologizes or admits mistakes. One quote in particular stings him: "Mark is currently the only C-level executive in this firm who has no hope of being CEO, for the simple reason that being CEO is the ultimate leadership role and no one would follow Mark."

The desire: Mark has tripped over the truth. (The 360 feedback provided a [1] clear insight, [2] compressed in time, and [3] discovered by the audience itself—that is, him.) The defensiveness he felt when he first started reading the feedback—"this is just sour grapes from jealous colleagues"—had crumbled by the end. He realizes his colleagues are right. He's been acting like a jerk. And he sees, too, that he has no hope of becoming a CEO—at his company or anywhere else—until he fixes himself. So he'll change. But how?

How Do We Create a Defining Moment?

What's the moment? There's no natural moment here, and that's part of the problem. The famous executive coach Marshall Goldsmith said that some of his clients do succeed in reforming their bad behavior—but no one notices! His clients had already imprinted themselves on their colleagues as jerks. So Goldsmith learned to press his clients to set up a meeting with their colleagues at which they would apologize for their behavior, promise to change, and ask their colleagues' help to do so. Taking a cue from Goldsmith, Mark schedules a meeting where he does exactly that. That's a defining moment—it marks a transition from the "old me" to the "new me."

Add ELEVATION:

1: Mark's meeting is not a peak—there's not much positive emotion involved. Nevertheless, the raw confessional nature of the meeting (a) *raises the stakes* and (b) *breaks the script,* which are two of the three traits of a moment of elevation.

Add INSIGHT:

1: Trip over the truth. The key moment of insight here is Mark's receipt of the 360 feedback—that is the first defining moment that leads to a second (the meeting).

2: Stretch for insight. The heart of the meeting is Mark's promise to reinvent himself. That's a risk for him—he wants to change but doesn't know if he's capable of it. (And frankly, his colleagues are skeptical.) Whether he succeeds or not, he will learn something about himself.

Add PRIDE:

1: Mark should take pride in the meeting itself—it takes courage to hold himself accountable for his own bad behavior. Beyond the meeting, he can lay the groundwork for *future* moments of pride.

2: Practice courage. Even as Mark asks for his colleagues' help, he knows it will be hard for them to speak up. It's hard to call someone a jerk to his face. Imagine if Mark equips his colleagues with a *language* of criticism: "I called you together today because I want this to be the moment when I stop acting like Old Mark—the jerk who doesn't listen—and start acting like New Mark. I'm going to try my hardest, but if you catch me acting like Old Mark, I'd really appreciate you calling me out." Why would that language help? Recall Mary Gentile's research about ethically troubling situations. Her contention is that what's hard about being courageous is not knowing *what* to do but rather knowing *how* to respond. Because of that, it's useful to preload our responses so we'll be ready in the moment. With the "Old Mark/New Mark" language, he is helping his colleagues preload their responses to the moments when he slips into his old behavior. (Hat tip to Tasha Eurich for this idea.)

3: Multiply milestones. Imagine if Mark sets a goal that he wants to take part in 10 meetings in a row without interrupting anyone—and asks his colleagues to police him. That might be a way to introduce some playfulness to an otherwise fraught situation, and if he hits the goal, it would be a moment well worth celebrating.

Add CONNECTION:

1: Deepen ties. Mark's meeting is a great example of showing vulnerability, which is a prerequisite to intimacy. When his colleagues see him lowering his guard, it allows them to see him as a human being with flaws—not a wholesale jerk.

2: Create shared meaning. The meeting provides a synchronizing moment; all his colleagues witness it together. It sharpens the demarcation point and reinforces the seriousness of Mark's pledge.

Final reflections: The key insight here is that an unpopular leader needs to create a moment. As Goldsmith says, even if a leader successfully changes his behavior, it might not fix his relationship problems, because his colleagues might not notice. The moment creates a reset point.

Moments of ELEVATION

Moments of INSIGHT

Moments of PRIDE

Moments of CONNECTION

Introduction to Moments of Connection

Think about the many defining moments we've encountered so far: Signing Day, the "reverse wedding" ceremony, the Trial of Human Nature, the Nashville lunch counter sit-ins, the CLTS open-defecation intervention, and the John Deere First Day Experience. As you know, they are moments of elevation, insight, and pride. But they are also *social* moments. They're more memorable because others are present.

Moments of connection deepen our relationships with others: You've known someone for only 24 hours, but you've already told them some of your deepest secrets. You endure a grueling experience with others and emerge with bonds that will never break. Your marriage hits a rocky patch—until one day your partner does something so thoughtful, you can't imagine loving anyone else.

Not all social moments are defining moments, of course. Think of the last PowerPoint presentation you witnessed at work during a team meeting—not, we predict, a peak moment of connection. So what is it about certain moments that *strengthen* relationships? And how do we create more of them?

We'll examine group relationships first: teams in organizations trying to rediscover their purpose, worshippers engaging in sacred rituals, and groups of friends laughing. (After the next chapter, you'll never think about laughter the same way again.) When members of groups grow closer, it's because of moments that *create shared meaning* (Chapter 10).

Then in Chapter 11 we'll study personal relationships, including the work of one psychologist who has identified a kind of "secret sauce" for effective relationships of all kinds: husbands and wives, businesses and clients, teachers and parents, doctors and patients. We'll also encounter the seemingly unthinkable: strangers who become fast friends in 45 minutes, as a result of following a carefully structured series of questions (which you can download for yourself).

In this final part of the framework, we'll study the unforgettable moments that connect us together.

10

Create Shared Meaning

1.

In 1998, Sonia Rhodes left the hospital with her recovering father, who had spent eight days there being treated for severe gastric bleeding. She felt profoundly grateful to the doctors and nurses who had saved his life. Yet she was unsettled by the experience he'd received as a patient.

He shared his cramped room with a stranger. Hospital staffers cycled in and out of the room, often without saying who they were. "Is that a doctor? Nurse? Food service staffer? Person who changes the linens? You had no idea," she said. They rarely introduced themselves—and it was rarer still for them to explain what they were doing.

In the midst of his recovery, her father suffered a fall that could have been prevented. A staffer had asked him to stand up even though he was woozy from receiving eight units of blood. Rhodes originally wanted to be by her dad's side to comfort him, but instead she was forced to be his protector: "I felt like as a family member, I was there to guard him from all the people who were coming in. 'Who are you? What's in your hand?'"

Most interactions with the hospital caregivers seemed to lack a basic human warmth. "They treated my dad like he was this old feeble person. . . . I wanted to tell them, 'He's a physicist and runs a company that makes satellites!'"

The experience had a profound impact on Rhodes, and not just because she was the daughter of a patient. She was also an executive at Sharp HealthCare, the system that managed the hospital where her father was treated. Advertisements for Sharp raved about the quality of care that patients could expect. In fact, the phone number on the ads—the one patients would call to inquire about treatment—was manned by her own team. After her father's experience, she wondered: *At Sharp, are we really who we say we are?*

She became an aggressive advocate for improving the patient experience—not the medical treatment, which was topnotch, but the *service* experience. She knew, she said, that fixing it would "define my career for the rest of my life."

For a year, she struggled to get attention for her ideas. Eventually, she had a critical meeting with Sharp's CEO, Michael Murphy. Although Murphy had spent most of his career on the financial side of the business, he had an instinct that Rhodes was right, and he committed himself to transforming Sharp. Murphy challenged his team to learn everything they could about how to deliver world-class service.

Over a period of about eight months, beginning in the fall of 2000, a team of executives including Murphy and Rhodes traveled together, visiting the stars of service experience: the Ritz-Carlton, Disney, General Electric, and Southwest Airlines. They consulted with experts: the Studer Group and coauthors James Gilmore and Joseph Pine (who wrote the seminal book *The Experience Economy*).

One consistent theme from the visits surprised them: You can't deliver a great patient experience without first delivering a great *employee* experience. And Sharp's "employee engagement" scores were weak compared with the likes of Ritz and Southwest.

Murphy and his executives had started the investigation focused narrowly on patients, but they now expanded their mission. They agreed on a new vision statement for Sharp:

To transform the health care experience and make Sharp:

- The best place for employees to work
- The best place for physicians to practice
- The best place for patients to receive care
- Ultimately, the best health care system in the universe

They called this vision the Sharp Experience. How would they get people to take it seriously, and not dismiss it as another flavor-of-the-month management scheme? They considered a "dog-and-pony" show in which a team of executives, including Murphy, would visit all of Sharp's health care facilities and share the new vision. But they realized it would take a year, realistically. "And by the time we got to the 30th place, the first place won't believe us anymore," Rhodes said.

Then someone suggested: Why don't we bring everyone together?

It seemed ludicrous. Sharp had 12,000 employees. There was no ballroom in San Diego that would fit all of them. And they could hardly put their patients' emergencies on hold (for the sake of discussing how to care for them better).

But the Sharp team kept talking and the answer took shape: They'd hold 3 separate sessions over 2 days, allowing them to fit comfortably in the San Diego Convention Center, while maintaining a core staff at all facilities to ensure that patients were not kept waiting. The logistics were daunting: Among other things, they would need to secure practically every available rental bus in San Diego. (In fact, they ended up bringing in buses from Los Angeles and even as far away as Arizona.)

On October 10, 2001, Sharp held its All-Staff Assembly. The hallways were jammed with Sharp employees who had arrived via bus, trolley, train, and boat. Murphy was pacing backstage nervously. "I'm not somebody who wants to go on a big stage," he said. But when he took the stage, he spoke candidly about the challenge ahead.

"This new journey will take courage," he said. "We are charting a different course because we believe we *must* in order to be the best." He urged his team to recommit to the passion and purpose that had led them to work in health care. And above all, he challenged them to act—to take ownership of the mission: "If we can take four steps in a process and reduce it to one, let's do it! If employees have great ideas for making something better, let's hear them! If a patient complains about something, let's make it a priority and fix it!"

Murphy shared the vision of the Sharp Experience: creating the best place for employees to work, for physicians to practice, and for patients to receive care—and "ultimately the best health care system in the universe." Some employees laughed at the audacity of the phrase, but his speech struck a chord. "We were used to getting changes through an email on Friday afternoon," said Kathy Rodean, a nurse who attended the All-Staff Assembly. But now here was Murphy saying, " 'This is our vision, and we want you to be part of it, to be able to get where we want to go.' That was such a different philosophy that it really, really brought people together."

After his speech, people were given the opportunity to volunteer for one of 100 "action teams" in areas such as employee satisfaction, patient satisfaction, and reward and recognition. The response was extraordinary: *1,600 people* volunteered—agreeing to shoulder extra work in support of the mission.

"When we finished that first session," Rhodes said, "people were crying, hugging, high-fiving . . . even the naysayers had tears in their eyes." One executive who had been skeptical of the event's value told her afterward, *We need to do this every quarter*.

In fact, they did decide to host another All-Staff Assembly the next year, and the next—it has become a cherished annual tradition.

That meeting started something big at Sharp. Fueled by the action teams, change seemed to happen on all fronts at once. Measurement systems changed, policies changed, habits changed. And as a result, the patient experience began to change. Sharp staffers found ways to deliver extraordinary service.

The landscaping crew had noticed that some patients didn't

receive visitors or flowers, so they started pruning roses, putting the blooms in a small bud vase, and walking them into the patients' rooms. (They called the program "This bud's for you.") Caregivers were trained to greet patients, introduce themselves, and explain their roles—solving the problem that had frustrated Rhodes during her father's stay. At Sharp Coronado Hospital, departing patients received a loaf of banana bread, "baked with love." And after they returned home, many patients were surprised to receive handwritten cards from the caregivers who had served them, thanking them for the chance to be part of their care.

In the five years following the first All-Staff Assembly, Sharp hospitals' unit patient satisfaction scores shot up in the national percentile rankings from as low as the teens to as high as the 90s. Physician satisfaction rose to the 80th percentile. Employee satisfaction rose by 13% and turnover declined by 14%. Net revenue increased by a half-billion dollars. In 2007, Sharp won the Malcolm Baldrige National Quality Award, the nation's highest presidential honor for quality and performance excellence.*

---

* In 2016, what would have been the 16th consecutive All-Staff Assembly was canceled in the face of a threatened strike by the nurses' union. In the end, the strike did not happen. Two observations: (1) A group of protesting nurses marched behind a banner reading "We Are the Sharp Experience." One of their demands was higher wages in order to retain the senior nurses who they argued were the best at delivering the Sharp Experience. Our best assessment is that the threatened strike reflected standard negotiating tactics rather than a rethinking of what Sharp had become over the preceding 15 years.(2) Moments of meaning matter. We would have counseled the leadership team to do everything possible to continue with the All-Staff Assembly despite the possibility of the strike—to treat it as sacred turf, in the same way that countries at odds will still compete together at the Olympics. The assembly is a moment of shared purpose. The welfare of patients should trump even a major disagreement among Sharp's players.

Did this transformation happen in a day at the convention center? Hardly. It took many years and the efforts of thousands of people. But the All-Staff Assembly was the first defining moment of the change.

And it was a moment with a character unlike others we've encountered. In the last section, we saw that moments of pride come when you distinguish yourself as an individual. As a result of achievements or courageous actions, *you* are made to feel *special*. But for groups, defining moments arise when we *create shared meaning*—highlighting the mission that binds us together and supersedes our differences. We are made to feel *united*.

How do you design moments that knit groups together? Sharp's leaders used three strategies: creating a synchronized moment, inviting shared struggle, and connecting to meaning. We'll explore all three and how they can be applied to groups ranging from religious devotees to lifeguards to janitors.

2.

Think of the last time you laughed in a group. Why were you laughing? The answer is pretty obvious: because someone said something funny.

Actually, that obvious answer is mostly wrong. The researcher Robert Provine and three assistants roamed around college campuses and city sidewalks, eavesdropping on conversations. When someone laughed, they jotted down what was said just before the laugh.

Provine found that fewer than 20% of the comments that sparked laughter were even remotely funny. In contrast to the jokes we laugh at from comedians, most laughter followed "banal remarks" such as "Look, it's Andre." Or "Are you sure?" Or "It was nice meeting you, too." Even the funniest remarks they recorded may not draw a chuckle from you: Two high-lights were "You don't have to drink, just buy us drinks" and "Do you date within your species?"

So why do we laugh? Provine found that laughter was 30 times more common in social settings than private ones. It's a *social* reaction. "Laughter is more about relationships than humor," Provine concluded. We laugh to tie the group to-gether. Our laughter says, *I'm with you. I'm part of your group.*

In groups, we are constantly assessing the reactions and feelings of the group. Our words and glances are a kind of so-cial sonar. *Are you still there? Are you hearing what I'm hearing? Are your reactions like mine?* Laughing in groups is another way of sending positive signals back and forth. We are synchroniz-ing our reactions.

This "synchronization" effect explains why it was so impor-tant to hold the Sharp All-Staff Assembly in person, with every-one together at the same moment (or as close to that ideal as they could get while still caring for patients). "The *magnitude* of an organization cannot ever be replicated via a memo," said Sonia Rhodes. "When you have 4,000 caregivers sitting in an audience who get up every day to help people's health care, to heal their lives, that's powerful. It's physical. . . . The hair on their bodies stood up. It was a shared experience."

The staffers who attended the All-Staff Assembly absorbed some critical messages from the situation: *This is important.* (Our leaders wouldn't rent all the buses in a city for something mundane.) *This is real.* (They can't back off the things they said when 4,000 of us heard them.) *We're in this together.* (I see a sea of faces around me, and we're all on the same team.) *And what we're doing matters.* (We've recommitted ourselves to a purpose—caring for those in need—that is bigger than any of us.)

Notice how many peak moments are, like the Sharp meeting, shared social moments: weddings, birthday parties, retirement celebrations, baptisms, festivals, graduations, rites of passage, concerts, competitions, and more. Or think about political rallies and marches—we crave the *personal* contact, the social reinforcement, even though it's with strangers. Occupying the streets together says: *This is important. This is real. We're in this together. And what we're doing matters.*

"Reasonable" voices in your organization will argue against synchronizing moments. It's too expensive to get everyone together. Too complicated. Couldn't we just jump on a webinar? Couldn't we just send the highlights via email? (Recall the Sharp nurse who said, "We were used to getting changes through an email on Friday afternoon.")

Remote contact is perfectly suitable for day-to-day communication and collaboration. But a big moment needs to be shared in person. (No one dials in to a wedding or graduation, after all.) The presence of others turns abstract ideas into social reality.

3.

The anthropologist Dimitris Xygalatas studied two rituals performed as part of the Hindu festival of Thaipusam on the island of Mauritius. In the milder, "low-ordeal" ritual, devotees prayed and chanted for several hours inside and outside a Hindu temple. In the "high-ordeal" ritual, devotees engaged in "body piercing with multiple needles and skewers, carrying heavy bamboo structures, and dragging carts attached by hooks to the skin for over 4 hours before climbing a mountain barefooted to reach the temple of Murugan."

Afterward, Xygalatas and his team offered both sets of people—low- and high-ordeal devotees—200 rupees (about two days' salary) to complete a questionnaire. Once they received the money, they were presented an opportunity to donate anonymously to the temple. The low-ordeal devotees donated an average of about 81 rupees. The high-ordeal devotees were substantially more generous, giving an average of 133 rupees, or two-thirds more than the low-ordeal group. More interesting still was the behavior of a third group of people, "high-ordeal observers"—people who had walked alongside the struggling high-ordeal followers but hadn't suffered physical hardship themselves. They were even more generous, giving an average of 161 rupees (or 80% of everything they received for the survey).

The researchers concluded that perceived pain increases "prosociality," or voluntary behavior to benefit others. They argued that extreme rituals—and specifically the shared experience of pain—can be seen as "social technology to bind in-groups together."

Such extreme rituals are at the far end of a spectrum that has, at its opposite end, corporate ropes courses, which simulate danger in order to spark bonding within work teams. On the surface, these experiences seem markedly different: One is horrific and psychologically unbearable, and the other is a sacred religious ritual. What they share is *struggle*.

If a group of people develops a bond quickly, chances are its members have been struggling together. One study found that when strangers were asked to perform a painful task together—in one case, submerging their hands in tubs of ice water to perform a "sorting task"—they felt a greater sense of bonding than did strangers who had performed the same task in room-temperature water. And this bonding happened even though the task was pointless! (Fraternity hazing is a good example of a pointless and painful bonding ritual.)

Imagine the bonding that emerges among people who struggle together at a task that *means something*: Activists fighting to protect a forest from clear-cutting. Start-up cofounders scrambling to meet the next payroll. Religious missionaries, in a distant part of the world, enduring daily rejection in the service of their faith.

What's the practical lesson here? Should we foist hardship on our employees for the sake of creating defining moments? Not quite. But it's worth observing that people will *choose* to struggle—not avoid it or resist it—if the right conditions are present. The conditions are: The work means something to them; they have some autonomy in carrying it out; and it's their choice to participate or not.

Those are the conditions that Sharp honored in calling for

volunteers to join "action teams" to improve the patient experience. The work was meaningful: serving patients better. The teams were given autonomy, often entrusted to formulate the health system's policies in a certain domain. Participation was voluntary. And volunteer they did: 1,600 people came forward. A mass movement of people willing to struggle together.

If you want to be part of a group that bonds like cement, take on a really demanding task that's deeply meaningful. All of you will remember it for the rest of your lives.

4.

To create moments of connection, we can bring people together for a synchronizing moment. We can invite them to share in a purposeful struggle. The final strategy centers on connecting them to a larger sense of meaning. In many organizations, our daily obligations—the emails, the meetings, the to-do lists—can numb us to the meaning of our work. And that sense of meaning can be the difference between a great performer and a mediocre one.

In his forthcoming book, *Great at Work: How Top Performers Work Less and Achieve More,* University of California, Berkeley professor Morten Hansen surveyed 5,000 employees and managers to understand the makeup of star performers. Among other findings, he discovered 17% of the employees "completely agreed" with this statement: "What I do at work makes a strong contribution to society, beyond making money." These people with a strong sense of meaning tended to have the highest performance rankings by their bosses.

In his research, Hansen also explored the distinction between *purpose* and *passion*. Purpose is defined as the sense that you are contributing to others, that your work has broader meaning. Passion is the feeling of excitement or enthusiasm you have about your work. Hansen was curious which would have the greater effect on job performance.

He grouped employees into categories. For instance, people who were low on passion *and* low on purpose were ranked by their bosses on average at the 10th percentile of performance:

	HIGH PURPOSE	LOW PURPOSE
HIGH PASSION		
LOW PASSION		10th percentile

That's lousy but not too surprising: If you are unenthusiastic about your job and feel it lacks meaning, you're not likely to overachieve. The opposite was true as well. When people had high passion *and* high purpose, they were stars:

	HIGH PURPOSE	LOW PURPOSE
HIGH PASSION	80th percentile	
LOW PASSION		10th percentile

Again, pretty predictable. But what if employees were strong on only one trait: passion *or* purpose? Who would perform better, the passionate or the purposeful? Let's start with the passionate:

	HIGH PURPOSE	LOW PURPOSE
HIGH PASSION	80th percentile	20th percentile
LOW PASSION		10th percentile

That's a shocking finding: People who were passionate about their jobs—who expressed high levels of excitement about their work—were still poor performers if they lacked a sense of purpose. And here's the final piece of the puzzle:

	HIGH PURPOSE	LOW PURPOSE
HIGH PASSION	80th percentile	20th percentile
LOW PASSION	64th percentile	10th percentile

The outcome is clear. Purpose trumps passion. Graduation speakers take note: The best advice is not "Pursue your passion!" It's "Pursue your purpose!" (Even better, try to combine both.)

Passion is individualistic. It can energize us but also isolate us, because my passion isn't yours. By contrast, purpose is something people can share. It can knit groups together.

How do you find purpose? Yale professor Amy Wrzesniewski, who studies how people make meaning of their work, said that many people believe they need to *find* their calling, as though it were a "magical entity that exists in the world waiting to be discovered." She believes purpose isn't discovered, it's *cultivated*.

Organizational leaders should learn to cultivate purpose — to unite people who might otherwise drift in different directions, chasing different passions. Purpose can be cultivated in a moment of insight and connection. Consider a study of lifeguards conducted by Adam Grant of Wharton. At a community recreation center in the Midwest, Grant divided 32 paid lifeguards into two groups. The first group, the Personal Benefit Group, read four stories that described how other lifeguards had benefited, down the road, from the skills they acquired on the job. The second group, the Meaning Group, read four stories about other lifeguards rescuing drowning swimmers.

The difference between the two groups was striking. The Meaning Group of lifeguards voluntarily signed up for 43% more hours of work in the weeks following the intervention. The stories had increased their interest in the work.

Furthermore, the lifeguards' supervisors, who did not know which set of stories the lifeguards had read, were asked to assess their "helping behavior" in the weeks that followed. Helping behaviors were defined as "actions taken voluntarily to benefit others." The Meaning Group's helping behavior increased by 21%. Meanwhile, there was no increase in helping behavior or hours worked by the Personal Benefit Group.

Keep in mind these differences in behavior were produced by nothing more dramatic than a 30-minute session, in which the lifeguards read four stories and talked about them. Truly a small-caps "defining moment." But its impact was real.

This intervention reflects a strategy we'll call "connecting to meaning"—finding ways to remind people of their purpose.

Similar interventions in other domains have been effective as well. When radiologists were shown photos of the patients whose X-rays they were scanning, they increased both the raw number and the accuracy of their scans. When nurses, assembling surgical kits, met a caregiver who would use the kits, they worked 64% longer than a control group and made 15% fewer errors. Connecting to meaning matters.

Not all of us save lives or serve patients. Sometimes purpose can be less tangible. What's the guiding "purpose" for the marketing collateral team or the server administrators or the benefits group in HR?

They all have a purpose, of course. Sometimes it's useful to keep asking, "Why?" Why do you do what you do? It might take several "Whys" to reach the meaning. For instance, consider a hospital janitor:

- Why do you clean hospital rooms? "Because that's what my boss tells me to do."
- Why? "Because it keeps the rooms from getting dirty."
- Why does that matter? "Because it makes the rooms more sanitary and more pleasant."
- Why does that matter? "Because it keeps the patients healthy and happy."

You know you're finished when you reach the *contribution*. Who is the beneficiary of your work, and how are you contributing to them? The janitor is making a contribution to the health and happiness of patients. The marketing collateral team might be making a contribution to the confidence and success of the field sales team. The benefits staffers might be making a contribution to the financial security and peace of mind of their fellow employees.

When you understand the ultimate contribution you're making, it allows you to transcend the task list. A hospital janitor's task list, for instance, is pretty concrete: Sweep, mop, scrub, sanitize, repeat. But understanding the purpose of the work allows for innovation and improvisation. One hospital janitor studied by Amy Wrzesniewski made it a point to strike up small talk with any patient who seemed to crave conversation. The janitor had realized that many patients had no one to talk to. That's purpose. "Combating patient loneliness" was not part of his task list, but it heightened the contribution he was making to patients' health and happiness.

A sense of purpose seems to spark "above and beyond" behaviors. At Sharp, as we saw, once employees had been reconnected with the meaning of their work, they began to push beyond their job descriptions to create extraordinary moments for patients. One patient with cancer was undergoing her fifth or sixth trial of chemotherapy, but she was not responding. She wanted to throw her pregnant daughter-in-law a baby shower but knew she would never make it out of the hospital before the baby was born. So the staff arranged for her to throw the shower at the hospital. They reserved a nice jade garden for her and encouraged her to decorate and organize the space as she liked.

"One of the last memories that her daughter-in-law will have is that before her mother-in-law died, she gave her a baby shower that she had planned," said Deborah Baehrens, manager of acute care at Sharp Memorial Hospital.

This was a remarkable moment for the patient, but imagine what it felt like for the staffers who made it happen. They came home that day feeling exhausted but fulfilled. *We did something that mattered today.*

That's a moment of shared meaning. It instills not the pride of individual accomplishment, but the profound sense of connection that comes from subordinating ourselves to a greater mission.

After the All-Staff Assembly in San Diego, after the shared laughter in the office, after the religious ritual in Mauritius, after the baby shower in the jade garden, people are connected tightly together as they realize that what they're doing is important and urgent and bigger than any of them.

11

Deepen Ties

1.

Stanton Elementary School in Washington, D.C., was a bad school. "It was the worst elementary school in one of the worst districts in the country, so it may have been the worst school in the country," said Susan Stevenson, former executive director of the education-focused Flamboyan Foundation.

In 2010, the school had performed so poorly that the district decided to "reconstitute" it, dismissing its principal and administrative team in order to start fresh. In June, 28-year-old Carlie John Fisherow was tapped to lead the turnaround.

She was sobered by what she saw as she walked the halls. Concrete cinder-block walls, massive heavy doors, grates on the windows, depressing stairwells, inadequate lighting, and everywhere a horrible shade of yellow paint, like dirty-teeth yellow. One teacher hired by Fisherow said, "It didn't remind me of a school at all. It reminded me of one of those sad orphanage stories."

Remodeling would have to wait. The first order of business was to manage the chaos that had been left in the wake of the district's takeover. The decision to turn over management of Stanton to Scholar Academies, which runs charter schools, had been announced very late in the school year. Many parents were furious because of the late notice and perceived lack of input. Teachers were angry and stunned because they'd had no idea that their jobs were in jeopardy.

Fisherow understood their anger, but she had very little time to soothe frustrations, because she had to make quick staffing decisions. During the last week of school, her team interviewed all the teachers and staff who worked at Stanton. The interviews, which took place in the school library, were frequently interrupted by kids "rocking bookshelves, calling each other names, picking up chairs and threatening to throw them at other kids," said Fisherow.

In the end, the school's new leadership team retained only 9 of the school's 49 employees. Once the new staff was on board, the team overhauled the depressing school environment: scrubbing it clean, lowering the ceilings for better sound, doubling the hallway lights, hanging college pennants and inspirational banners everywhere, and adding some fresh Kelly-green paint.

When Stanton's students walked through the door on the first day of school in fall 2010, they walked into what was effectively a new school. It had a new principal, a new staff, a new curriculum, and a new paint job. Fisherow and her team were confident that, even in a year's time, they could make a big difference for their students.

But shortly after classes began, they realized just how hard the turnaround would be. In the first week of school, Fisherow was introduced to a new term, *elopement*, which referred to students leaving their classrooms without permission. Elopement was epidemic at Stanton. Many classrooms at the school had two swinging doors, like a western saloon, and Fisherow said, "Kids would walk out one side and back in the other. They'd circle in and out of their classrooms all day long . . . into the hallway, to the dark stairwells, down to the cafeteria, into the gym. . . ."

The staff could not get control over the school. An astonishing 321 suspensions were enforced during that first year, with many of those going to the same subset of misbehaving students. 28% of all the students were classified as "truant," meaning they had missed 10 or more days of school without an excuse.

"The year was crazy. It was like being in the trenches. We felt like we were in battle," said Fisherow. None of their plans were working. As one observer said of Stanton, during the 2010–11 school year "the school went from 'really bad' to 'worse.'" Then, midway through the year, Fisherow fell down the stairs at school and broke her leg.

"By the spring, we were ready to do anything," said Fisherow. "We were desperate to do something different. When you're down and out, you're open to all sorts of ideas."

Looking for solutions, Fisherow met with a representative

from the Flamboyan Foundation, a family foundation focused on improving schools. Flamboyan was known for its emphasis on "family engagement"—encouraging parents to play a more active and supportive role in their children's education. Fisherow knew that this was a weak spot at Stanton. "You can paint and put in lighting and college pennants, and bring in a great team, but if there's not trust with the people you're serving, it doesn't matter," she said.

There was a history of mistrust between parents and teachers in the D.C. school system. Susan Stevenson, the foundation's executive director, convened focus groups with 150 families from across the district. "What we learned was really disheartening," she said. The parents thought teachers were ineffective and indifferent—just there to collect a paycheck. Many of the parents had attended D.C. public schools themselves, and they were often bitter about their own educational experience.

Teachers felt the parents didn't seem to value education. They rarely showed up to events at school. It was tough to get them to show up for a parent-teacher conference about their own child. (Meanwhile, the parents had concluded essentially the opposite—they perceived the teachers as uninterested in their kids. So it didn't seem worth the time to attend events or meetings.)

Stevenson had learned of a program in Sacramento, California, that was designed to boost parental involvement. It had shown promising results in early tests, and she wanted to pilot the program in D.C. with a handful of schools. Fisherow said that "we basically begged Flamboyan to take us on as a pilot school."

Late in the school year, Fisherow called together the faculty to hear how the pilot program would work. She was nervous: "My staff was tired, really tired, at that point. A two-hour training on a Thursday night . . . I thought, *There's no way this is gonna go well.*"

At the meeting, the foundation's advisors unveiled the activity that would be at the heart of their plan: a "home visit," in which teachers would go to see parents, before the next school year started, to talk about their children.

The concept of a "home visit" was not unfamiliar to the teachers. Many charter schools, for instance, require home visits. But often the goal of these home visits is to ask parents to sign a "contract" in which they pledge to support their kids in certain ways.

The Flamboyan Foundation's approach to home visits was quite different. The teachers were forbidden to bring any paper to the visits—no contracts to sign, no information to review. Their role was simply to ask questions and listen to the answers. Those questions were prescribed for them:

"Tell me about your child's experiences in school. Tell me about yours."

"Tell me your hopes and dreams for your child's future."

"What do you want your child to be someday?"

"What do I need to do to help your child learn more effectively?"

One teacher who was there that night, a fourth-grade math instructor named Melissa Bryant, said, "My first reaction was 'I call bullshit.'" Bryant had taught in some tough neighborhoods even before she got to Stanton—South Philly, Harlem,

Bedford-Stuyvesant—and she was skeptical that one home visit was going to accomplish anything.

But then two parents spoke. Flamboyan had flown them out from Sacramento, where they'd received home visits as part of the program there. They talked about what the visits had meant to them: It was the first time anyone had asked them about *their* dreams for their kids. Usually, when the school came calling, there was a form to fill out, or a discipline problem to talk about, or a request for volunteer time. But the home visit was different. The teacher was on their couch, *listening to them.*

Hearing the parents, Bryant's attitude changed. "We say we value parents' voices, but we never *really* listen to them," she said. "It gave me goose bumps. I thought, *Wow, we need to do more.*"

Flamboyan's research suggested that home visits could have profound effects on the parents' engagement, which in turn could boost student outcomes. "It was a like a light went off in the room," Fisherow said. "We thought, *This can have a huge impact* AND *we can do this.*"

About 15 teachers agreed to conduct home visits that summer. The early progress was slow—parents were skeptical at first. But then a positive buzz about the visits began to spread around the community. "Parents were *wanting* visits," Bryant said. "You'd hear them saying, 'Did you get a home visit? I got a home visit.'" One teacher was stopped on the street by a parent who was annoyed that she hadn't had her home visit yet.

On the first day of school in the fall of 2011, the vibe at Stanton was palpably different. For one thing, many of the students already knew their teachers' faces and names—they'd seen them in their own living rooms, talking to their mothers. And that basic familiarity and trust resulted in better behavior. One day, an issue in the cafeteria resulted in about 100 students having to line up on the stairs. The previous year, there would have been pandemonium. This year, there was silence and order.

"Our school *felt like* a school instantaneously," Fisherow said. "I could not believe that it had worked so fast."

The true jaw-dropping moment, though, happened a month into the school year, at the annual "Back to School" night. The parents were invited to come to the school, meet their kids' teachers, and see their classrooms. Usually, Bryant said, the parental participation was underwhelming: "Every year—not just at Stanton, but at every school I've ever been in—that was just a day to clean my room. Nobody shows up except for the same three parents, and you've already talked to them because they come to everything."

Only 25 parents had shown up the previous year. This year, optimistic that the family visits would make a difference, the staff set up 50 seats in the auditorium.

Fifteen minutes before the program was supposed to begin, all 50 seats were full. So they added another 100. In 10 more minutes, to their amazement, all those seats filled up, too. The faculty had been sitting, so they vacated their seats to make room for more parents. When Fisherow finally took the stage to welcome the crowd, it was standing room only. More than 200 parents had come to the school!

"There was a moment where all of us looked at each other," said Bryant. "We felt like we were in *The Twilight Zone*."

The astonishing moments continued, one after another. At-tendance at parent-teacher conferences spiked from 12% of parents the previous year to 73% in 2011-12. Truancy dropped from 28% to 11%. Academic performance improved, too: The number of students rated "proficient" at reading on the DC Comprehensive Assessment System (CAS) test doubled from 9% to 18%, and proficiency at math tripled from 9% to 28%. Suspensions went virtually extinct, from 321 to 24.

Nor did the family engagement reflect a brief "honeymoon period." It actually strengthened with time. Year over year, the successes built: More home visits. More parental participation. Better behavior. Higher test scores. By the 2013–14 school year, Stanton's CAS proficiency scores had climbed to 28% in reading and 38% in math.

A typical third grader in Washington, D.C., might spend 7 hours per day in school, across a calendar of 180 school days. That's 1,260 hours of school time. The impact of a one-hour home visit should have been hopelessly diluted. Yet that one hour made a difference that rippled across the whole year. That's a defining moment.

How could such a small intervention have such a big ef-fect? We are accustomed to thinking about relationships in terms of time: The longer the relationship endures, the closer it must grow. But relationships don't proceed in steady, predict-able increments. There's no guarantee that they will deepen with time. When you and your uncle make the same small talk every Thanksgiving, it's not a surprise that 10 years later, you don't feel any closer. Conversely, have you ever met someone and felt instantly that you liked and trusted them?

What we'll see is that, if we can create the right kind of moment, relationships can change in an instant. That's what happened at Stanton, and it can happen in other relationships at work and at home.

What is it about certain moments that deepens our ties to others?

2.

The social psychologist Harry T. Reis has spent his career studying that mystery. In 2007, he published a provocative paper called "Steps Toward the Ripening of Relationship Science." It's a modest title for what is, in reality, an attempt to climb a kind of academic Everest.

Reis challenges his fellow researchers to work toward a universal theory to explain relationships. Why do some relationships endure while others crumble? Why does intimacy develop between some partners and not others? What, in short, is the "circuitry" of a successful relationship?

Reis presents his candidate for the "central organizing principle" of relationship science—a concept that could tie together the vast and scattered research literature. It can be captured in one sentence: Our relationships are stronger when we *perceive* that our *partners* are *responsive* to us. (The term used frequently is "perceived partner responsiveness.")

Responsiveness encompasses three things:

Understanding: My partner knows how I see myself and what is important to me.

Validation: My partner respects who I am and what I want.

Caring: My partner takes active and supportive steps in helping me meet my needs.

Notice how much of the recipe is about *attunement*. We want our partners to see us the way we see ourselves, and we want them to accept us and to help us get what we want. It's incredibly selfish, frankly—me, me, me! It's reciprocal selfishness, actually, since our partner expects the same.

What does nonresponsiveness look like? You walk in the door, distraught, and your partner doesn't even notice (anti-understanding). When you describe a new interest or passion, your partner seems uninterested or dismissive (anti-validation). In a situation where a hug or a soothing comment would go a long way, you get a blank face (anti-caring). Nonresponsiveness is corrosive. It deprives us of our individuality; we're not seen or treated as special.*

Studies show that responsive treatment leads infants to feel secure and children to feel supported; it makes people more

---

* For another example of nonresponsiveness, look no further than your teenager. You say something and your teen either doesn't notice or seems not to be able to translate your clear instructions into coherent action (anti-understanding). When you try to clarify what you're asking for, the teen rolls his eyes (anti-validation). In a situation where a neutral "Okay, got it" would go a long way, you get the summary statement, "Whatever!" ("Whatever" is anti-everything.)

satisfied with their friends; and it brings couples closer together. Responsiveness is correlated with attachment security, self-esteem, emotional well-being, and a laundry list of other positive attributes (even healthier levels of diurnal cortisol, which sounds like a Harry Potter spell but is actually a stress hormone).

So when we ask what made the home visits at Stanton Elementary School so effective, the answer is simple: responsiveness. Take a second look at those four questions that the teachers asked the parents:

> "Tell me about your child's experiences in school. Tell me about yours." (*Understanding*)
>
> "Tell me your hopes and dreams for your child's future." (*Validation*)
>
> "What do you want your child to be someday?" (*Validation*)
>
> "What do I need to do to help your child learn more effectively?" (*Caring*)

Remember that the Flamboyan Foundation forbade the teachers to bring documents to the visits. Now it's clear why: Generic documents are depersonalizing. *Here's the same pamphlet we're handing to everyone.* Responsiveness is not compatible with a canned agenda.

Reis was right about the vast reach of the responsiveness concept. In the business world, the Gallup organization has developed a set of questions to assess employees' satisfaction at work. Gallup has found that positive responses to the questions are associated with almost all the goals a typical manager would

care about: the employee's engagement, retention, productiv-
ity, and profitability—even the satisfaction of the organization's
customers. Gallup discovered that the six most revealing questions are the ones below. Notice that the final three of them
might as well have been penned by Reis himself:

1. Do I know what is expected of me at work?
2. Do I have the materials and equipment I need to do
   my work right?
3. Do I have the opportunity to do what I do best every
   day?
4. In the last seven days, have I received recognition or
   praise for good work? (*Validation.*)
5. Does my supervisor, or someone at work, seem to care
   about me as a person? (*Caring.*)
6. Is there someone at work who encourages my
   development? (*Understanding. Caring.*)

Remember Keith Risinger, the sales manager who coached
Bob Hughes on better listening and later awarded him the Bose
headphones to celebrate his progress? He's a good example of
a responsive manager. He pays attention to his team members,
invests time in them, and recognizes their successes. As the
Gallup research suggests, responsiveness matters as much at
work as it does at home.

The concept has similar potency in the health care system.
Responsiveness is becoming an *expected* part of patient care.
Health systems around the world (such as Sharp from the last
chapter) have made more respectful treatment of patients an
institutional priority.

The Institute for Healthcare Improvement (IHI), a non-profit best known for its lifesaving work reducing errors and infections in hospitals, has in recent years led the charge for patient-centered care. The former CEO of the IHI, Maureen Bisognano, had a personal connection to the topic. Bisognano, the oldest of nine siblings, had a younger brother named Johnny. He was handsome and smart, and as a teenager he loved his side job as a ball boy for the Boston Celtics.

When he was 17, he was diagnosed with Hodgkin's disease. The disease progressed quickly, and for several years Johnny was in and out of hospitals. Maureen visited often, and she remembers the parade of doctors through his room. "They'd speak over him, and about him, but almost never to him," she said.

When Johnny was 20, his illness was in its final stages. He came to Maureen's apartment and told her, "I'm not gonna make it." She didn't know what to say or do. "He was ready to face death, but I wasn't," she said.

In that era—before hospice care became common—even a dying patient received intrusive care. (*Especially* a dying patient.) Johnny spent most of his time in hospitals being monitored and probed and treated by caregivers who were well intentioned but unresponsive—they never got around to asking for *his* perspective.

Until one day at Peter Bent Brigham Hospital (now Brigham and Women's Hospital), when a physician came to visit. Maureen was sitting at Johnny's bedside. The physician turned to her brother and said, "Johnny, what do *you* want?"

"I want to go home," Johnny answered.

What happened next astounded Maureen. The physician

asked for her jacket. He took it from her and draped it around Johnny, then carried him from the hospital bed to her car.

Johnny returned to his family home, and he spent his final days in the company of the people who loved him most. He died a few days after his 21st birthday.

Decades later, Maureen Bisognano read an article in the *New England Journal of Medicine* that reminded her of her brother's experience. The authors, Michael J. Barry and Susan Edgman-Levitan, had written: "Clinicians, in turn, need to relinquish their role as the single, paternalistic authority and train to become more effective coaches or partners—learning, in other words, how to ask, 'What matters to you?' as well as 'What is the matter?'"

That question "What matters to you?" struck Bisognano like a lightning bolt. It was, at heart, the same question the compassionate physician had asked her brother. It was also a question—she now realized—that captured the essence of patient-centered care. In speeches before hundreds of caregivers, she would appeal to them to ask their patients, "not just 'What's the matter?' but 'What matters to you?'" It was a rallying cry for more responsiveness.

The question caught on immediately with many doctors and nurses. After hearing Bisognano speak in Paris in 2014, one nurse, Jen Rodgers, from a pediatric unit in Scotland, took the question home with her. She gave construction paper and markers to the children on her ward and encouraged them to draw on a page titled "What Matters to Me."

One of those kids was Kendra, seven, who had just checked into the children's ward for surgery. She had autism and had never spoken a word. Her father was with her to help her communicate with the staff.

But within 24 hours after Kendra checked in, her father suffered a suspected cardiac arrest. He had to be rushed to another hospital, leaving Kendra alone, terrified, and unable to speak for herself.

But she had completed her "What Matters to Me" page, and it opened a door into her world. "My name is Kendra," she wrote. "I have autism. I can't speak so I won't be able to if it hurts. I don't like medicine by my mouth so watch out I will struggle. I love to feel people's hair, it is my way of saying hello." (See her drawing on the next page.)

Her nurses used her drawing as a guidebook for caring for her. Without it, Rodgers said, the nurses could have easily misinterpreted her behavior. Imagine them dealing with a hard-to-understand child who grabs at their hair and fights when given oral medication. She might have been deemed aggressive. She might have been confined to her room, which would have caused her even more stress.

Her father recovered quickly and rejoined her within a few days. In the meantime, the nurses had looked after Kendra by honoring her requests. They comforted her. ("I love cuddles to reassure me," she'd written.) They avoided oral medications when possible, knowing she didn't like it. They high-fived her. They let her feel their hair, and they combed hers. ("My dad is rubbish at doing my hair.") Their relationship was utterly transformed because of a simple question: "What matters to you?"

Rodgers said that the experience with Kendra convinced some of her skeptical colleagues that the question was worth asking every time. Today, the "What matters to you?" drawing has become standard practice for every children's ward in Scotland.

And because of the advocacy of Maureen Bisognano and the IHI, that responsive question has been embraced by doctors and nurses around the world. As we saw with the Stanton home visits, with the right kind of moment, relationships can change in an instant.

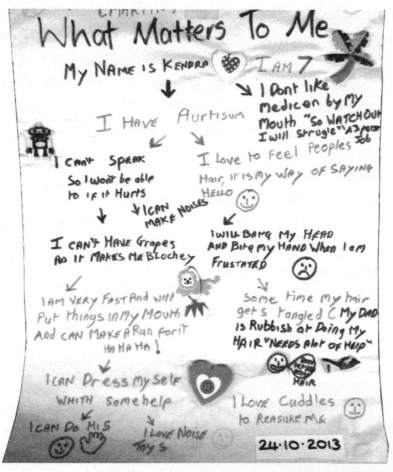

3.

Responsiveness matters in the complex, emotional relationships between caregivers and patients, but it also plays a role in more mundane, day-to-day interactions. When you find yourself infuriated by poor service, for instance, chances are it's because of a lack of responsiveness. You are seated at a restaurant table and no one acknowledges you for 10 minutes. You are asked at the car rental counter whether you want to buy extra insurance, even though you never have. You wait on hold for a long time and, when a representative finally answers, you are *challenged to prove your identity.*

Here's your authors' pet peeve: We book a lot of flights, and we always sort the results by duration. (We want the shortest.) For almost twenty years, we've been sorting by duration. Yet not once has any travel website stored our preference. Meanwhile, Chip accidentally clicked on a Hello Kitty link months ago, and he is still being stalked around the Internet by ads for cute-kitten luggage. Why does the Internet have a photographic memory for ad clicks and amnesia about what we actually care about?

What links these annoyances, of course, is the lack of understanding, validation, and caring. We hate being treated impersonally: *You are not special. You're a number.*

Analysts at the Corporate Executive Board (CEB) studied customer service calls and the ratings that customers provided afterward. To the researchers' surprise, only half of the customers' ratings were attributable to the particular call they had just experienced. The other half reflected the way they had been treated previously. (For instance, if the customer had made six previous calls to get an issue resolved, then it didn't matter if the seventh was handled brilliantly.)

The CEB team called the customers' memory of previous treatment their "baggage." Most call center reps had the instinct to *avoid* the customer's baggage. If they saw in the records that the customer had been passed around a lot, they wouldn't mention it. Why bring it up? It's like pouring salt on the wound, they figured. Better just to resolve the issue as quickly as possible.

So the CEB ran a set of studies on the art of "baggage handling." At one call center, the researchers assigned reps at random either to ignore customer baggage or to address it. For instance, let's say that a customer had called repeatedly about battery problems with a new tablet computer. Compare the responses of the reps:

BAGGAGE-IGNORING REP NO. 1: Thanks for your purchase. I understand that you are having a problem with the battery. Let's start from the beginning by going to the "Settings" section on your tablet to make sure that you are not using any feature that is draining your battery more quickly than normal.

BAGGAGE-HANDLING REP NO. 2: Thanks for your purchase. I understand that you are having a problem with the battery. . . . Hmm, according to our system, it looks like you've called several times about this, is that right? Okay, thanks. Can you tell me what you have tried already, and what has or has not worked to help preserve the battery life? Then we can take it from there instead of repeating stuff you've already tried.

Baggage handling is responsive: It demonstrates under-standing and validation of a customer's frustrating past experi-ence. And the effect it had on calls was stunning: Customers rated the quality of their experience with Rep No. 2 almost twice as highly as the other, and their perceptions of the effort they had to invest to resolve the problem plummeted by 84%.

In his landmark paper on responsiveness, Harry Reis had set out to explain a "central organizing principle" of relation-ships. His primary focus was on what makes personal bonds stronger. But we've seen the broad reach of the principle: It can explain not just what makes partners happier in a marriage, but also what makes employees feel noticed and valued, what makes patients feel respected in their treatment, and even what makes customers satisfied with a support call.

If we want more moments of connection, we need to be more responsive to others.

4.

Responsiveness doesn't necessarily lead to intimacy. The bag-gage-handling phone reps were responsive, after all, but there weren't any tearful goodbyes at the end of the call. When re-sponsiveness is coupled with openness, though, intimacy can develop quickly.

Here's how it happens: One person reveals something and waits to see if the other person will share something back. The reciprocity, if it comes, is a sign of understanding, validation, and caring. *I've heard you, I understand and accept what you're saying, and I care for you enough to disclose something about myself.* An unresponsive partner—like a seatmate on a flight who puts on his headphones shortly after you make a comment—terminates the reciprocity, freezing the relationship.

This turn-taking can be incredibly simple. In one study conducted at a bus stop, a researcher approached strangers with one of two canned comments. The "low-intimacy" comment was, "Well, my day is over. How about yours?"

The "high-intimacy" comment shows how easy it can be to initiate the cycle of turn-taking. All the researcher had to say was, "I'm really glad this day is over—I've had a really hectic day. How about you?" That's the *high*-intimacy comment! On that scale, a handshake would probably be X-rated. Even so, that tiny bit of self-disclosure sparked significantly more intimate comments in return.

> EXPERIMENTER: I'm really glad this day is over—I've had a really hectic day. How about you?
> SUBJECT (young woman): No, I had a great day.
> EXPERIMENTER: You had a great day?
> SUBJECT: Oh, a beautiful day. I went out with someone I really liked, so I had a great day.

In this scenario, the experimenter reveals something personal, the subject reciprocates, and the experimenter responds further, deepening the exchange. It's intimacy in steps. Surely we all have a relationship with the opposite dynamic, where our responses might as well be programmed: "Working hard, Dave?" "Nah, hardly working." "I hear that." "Another day, another dollar." "Yup." "Okay, see you." That's a relationship on a permanent plateau.

Intimacy escalates with turn-taking. For a dramatic example of this, consider a study by the social psychologist Art Aron and four colleagues called "The Experimental Generation of Interpersonal Closeness." (Which, by the way, would have been a great alternate name for *The Bachelor*.*)

In the study, some college students taking a psychology class volunteered to be paired up with another student in the class who was a stranger to them. Each pair was given 36 numbered questions on slips of paper in an envelope, to be drawn one at a time and answered by both people.

The exercise was divided into three rounds of 15 minutes each. As they progressed, the questions became increasingly intimate. Here are three sample questions from each round:

ROUND 1

Question 1: Given the choice of anyone in the world, whom would you want as a dinner guest?

Question 4: What would constitute a "perfect" day for you?

Question 8: Name three things you and your partner appear to have in common.

---

* Jokes aside, *The Bachelor* and similar shows are masterful at whipping up instant love (moments of connection), for reasons that we are about to see. But note how easily the producers conjure moments of elevation: There is beautiful scenery and delicious food (sensory appeal), plus novel experiences (breaking the script) and competitive excitement (raising the stakes). It's classic peak-building.

ROUND 2

Question 13: If a crystal ball could tell you the truth about yourself, your life, the future, or anything else, what would you want to know?

Question 15: What is the greatest accomplishment of your life?

Question 21: What roles do love and affection play in your life?

ROUND 3

Question 26: Complete this sentence: "I wish I had someone with whom I could share . . . "

Question 28: Tell your partner what you like about them; be very honest this time, saying things that you might not say to someone you've just met.

Question 33: If you were to die this evening with no opportunity to communicate with anyone, what would you most regret not having told someone? Why haven't you told them yet?

At the conclusion, the pair were separated and asked to complete a short survey that included the IOS (Inclusion of Other in the Self) scale, which is a measure of closeness. The mean IOS score of the participants was 3.82; the scale has a maximum of 7.

How high is 3.82? Consider that researchers asked another group of students on campus to rate their "closest, deepest, most involved, and most intimate relationship"—possibly their girlfriend or boyfriend or mother or best friend—on the same

IOS scale. And 30% of those students rated their "most intimate relationship" at *less than* 3.82.

Think about that. Two strangers sat down and had 45 minutes of conversation. That's a quick lunch or a long tech support call. Yet at the end of it, they felt as close to that stranger as 30% of college students feel to *the most intimate relationship in their lives*!

That's interpersonal alchemy.

Art Aron's 36 questions have become famous—there's even an app you can download if you want to try them out with a partner. (It's called "36 Questions.") But in some ways, the questions are beside the point. It's not these specific questions that create intimacy—it's the turn-taking. Another set of 36 questions could work just as well, so long as they matched the escalating cycle of vulnerability that Aron created.

The critical realization, however, is that *this cycle will not begin naturally*. You must start it.

To explore this further, we challenged a group of readers as follows: "Sometime in the next week, when you're having a conversation with a friend or family member, push intentionally beyond small talk. Share something real—maybe it's a challenge/struggle you're facing at home or work. Make yourself vulnerable and trust that your partner will reciprocate, allowing you to take the conversation to a higher level."

People were amazed at the response they got. Here's one account from a man named Mike Elam:

> *I had a conversation with a fellow manager at the office that started as a project update meeting, but I did go*

deeper than the project with the discussion. Prior to this meeting, we were strictly peers at work and really knew very little about each other beyond our roles at the company. I found that she was actually relocating to the Phoenix area later this year and would be continuing to work on the project remotely. The reason for the relocation was health issues with her spouse. We then talked about those issues because he has multiple sclerosis and was having issues getting around in the winter here and in their multistory house, so they decided to move. Then we discussed the trials and tribulations with getting their current home ready to sell and the process of packing to move, etc.

The first question didn't need to be too deep or personal but it was like "peeling an onion" where we were going just slightly deeper on each exchange and when finished, we had moved quite a bit. The exercise totally changed the dynamics of my work discussions and relationship with this person.

Relationships don't deepen naturally. In the absence of action, they will stall. As Elam said above, "we were strictly peers at work and really knew very little about each other beyond our roles at the company." That's a frozen relationship. But, as we've seen, acting with responsiveness to others can create tighter bonds: bonds between teachers and parents, doctors and patients, call center reps and customers, colleagues at work, and even strangers in a lab experiment. And those bonds can continue to strengthen with astonishing speed.

A defining moment of connection can be both brief and extraordinary.

MOMENTS OF CONNECTION
THE WHIRLWIND REVIEW

1. Moments of connection bond us with others. We feel warmth, unity, empathy, validation.

2. To spark moments of connection for groups, we must create shared meaning. That can be accomplished by three strategies: (1) creating a synchronized moment; (2) inviting shared struggle; and (3) connecting to meaning.
   - *Sharp's recommitment to the customer experience had all three elements: (1) the All-Staff Assembly; (2) the voluntary "Action Teams"; and (3) a call for dramatic improvements in the way customers were cared for.*

3. Groups bond when they struggle together. People will welcome a struggle when it's their choice to participate, when they're given autonomy to work, and when the mission is meaningful.
   - *Xygalatas's study of religious devotees concludes that the shared experience of pain can be seen as "social technology to bind in-groups together."*

4. "Connecting to meaning" reconnects people with the purpose of their efforts. That's motivating and encourages "above and beyond" work.
   - *Hansen's research: When it comes to performance, strong purpose trumps strong passion.*

5. In individual relationships, we believe that relationships grow closer with time. But that's not the whole story. Sometimes long relationships reach plateaus. And with the right moment, relationships can deepen quickly.
   - *Fisherow and her team turned around the troubled Stanton Elementary School by relying, in part, on short parent-teacher home visits before the start of school.*

6. According to the psychologist Harry Reis, what deepens individual relationships is "responsiveness": mutual understanding, validation, and caring.
   - *Stanton's teachers showed responsiveness by listening to parents' hopes for their kids.*
   - *In health care, caregivers are switching from the question "What's the matter?" to "What matters to you?"*
   - *"Baggage-handling" customer service reps validate customers' past experiences.*

7. Responsiveness coupled with openness leads to intimacy. It happens via "turn-taking."
   - *Art Aron's 36 Questions experiment leads total strangers to become intimate—in 45 minutes!*

Clinic 5
How Can You Combat the "Silo" Mentality?

The situation: At dinner, the VP of sales and the VP of market-ing of a large company have finally acknowledged something they've both known for a long time: Their departments have a dysfunctional relationship. Although marketing and sales should work hand in hand, their teams have been operating in silos. The marketing team creates slick promotional materials and adver-tising, and the sales team complains that the materials don't re-flect how customers think about the company's products. Sales insists that the products would sell better at a lower price, but marketing scoffs that the sales team is just chasing a quick deal rather than having deeper conversations about the product's virtues. Although this story is fictional, similar conflicts are all too common.

The desire: The executives are fed up with the lack of col-laboration. Their teams aren't at war, really—they are just too comfortable staying in their own spheres. The two leaders are determined to get their teams working together more effec-tively, but they know it will require a shock to the system.

How Do We Create a Defining Moment?

What's the moment? The moment needs to be created. The VPs schedule a two-day off-site meeting. The question is: How can they design a meeting that becomes a defining moment for their teams?

Add ELEVATION:

1: Break the script. The off-site meeting itself breaks the script. It's a change of environment, a disruption of routines.

2: Boost sensory appeal, raise the stakes. When the meeting begins, participants are led outside to an actual Formula One racing car in the parking lot. Teams are formed—with sales and marketing intermixed—and trained to act as a "pit crew." The teams compete to see who can change the car's tires most quickly. With each attempt, the teams get better and better at collaborating. It's pure fun. By the end, the teams are laughing and clowning—but deadly serious when it's their time to act as the pit crew. Afterward, back in the meeting room, the teams discuss their experience and what it means for effective collaboration.

Add INSIGHT:

1: Trip over the truth. The leaders surprise the group by inviting a customer to address them. The customer discusses the "whiplash" effect of interacting with the marketing and sales teams. "It's like I'm talking to two different companies," he says.

2: Trip over the truth and stretch for insight. Prior to the off-site, two marketers and two salespeople were "embedded" with the other team for a week. Then, at the off-site meeting, they share what they learned: The marketers embedded in sales present, "What marketing doesn't understand about sales," and their counterparts present, "What sales doesn't understand about marketing."

Add PRIDE:

1: Recognize others. The departments have not worked well together in general, but there have been exceptions. The people who made those bright spots happen are given a Team Chemistry Award—a pack of Mentos and a jug of Diet Coke. (If that combo seems puzzling, Google it.) After the meeting, the two VPs keep a supply of Mentos and Diet Coke stashed in their offices so they can give out more awards spontaneously when their teams earn it.

2: Practice courage. One reason why the sales and marketing teams don't collaborate is that their communication tends to be passive-aggressive. They are polite to each other when they're face-to-face; later, they complain to their colleagues and drag their feet. So at the off-site, people practice "crucial conversations." The session is such a hit that the term *crucial conversation* becomes a kind of inside joke. Back at the office, people will often approach each other by saying, "Could we have a crucial conversation?" (But it's only half-joking, since the humor defuses the difficulty of starting the discussion.)

3: Multiply meaningful milestones. The two teams set goals for themselves—moments they will celebrate. The moments they choose include: (1) the first time a sales staffer trades more emails in a week with the marketing team than with the sales team; (2) the first time someone from either group lobbies for the other to get more resources; and (3) the first time someone solves a problem for the other team.

Add CONNECTION:

1: Note that many of the activities already discussed would be effective at creating connections, including the pit crew experience, the embed presentations, and the "crucial conversations" practice. Often the same "moment" will include more than one element of a defining moment.

2: Create shared meaning. The act of holding the off-site is itself a powerful signal. Bringing everyone physically together, outside the office, sends the message: *We are in this together.* It's a synchronized moment.

3: Create shared meaning. At the conclusion of the meeting, the executives challenge their teams to collaborate on a plan for approaching an important client prospect. They must formulate the plan and present it to the two vice presidents in two hours. It's a difficult mission—but it's precisely the difficulty that helps to bond the team members **to each other.**

Final reflections: The two things we want to highlight about this case: (1) Creating a moment is critical in a complex, political situation like this. The moment is a demarcation point where you announce: Before this retreat, we were siloed. After this retreat, we commit to working together. The shared context gives the goal social momentum: *If I behave badly, you can call me on it because you know that I know I committed to do better.* (2) The reason many people hate meetings is that emotion is deliberately squeezed out. Participants sit and listen to programmed presentations. But this is a choice, not an inevitability. You can just as easily conduct a meeting that has drama, meaning, and connection. You cannot bring two teams together by simply talking about unity. They must *experience* unity. That's what makes it a defining moment.

12

Making Moments Matter

1.

Once you realize how important moments can be, it's easy to spot opportunities to shape them. Take a high school student waiting for her college admissions decisions. Years ago, the decisions would arrive in the mail; now they're as likely to come via email. But her emotions are the same. When the moment comes, her stomach churns. She takes a deep breath, opens the letter, and scans frantically for key words and phrases, and—there it is!—the sweet word *Congratulations*! She lets out a shout of delight and reads it again. Seven times.

That's a great moment of pride and elevation. But, let's be honest, the university deserves very little credit for making the moment matter. A letter? An email? That's the best they can do? Keep in mind that, for teenagers, the waiting game is a classic time of transition. How could we heighten the peak?

Just by applying the tools in this book, we can come up with many suggestions:

- Include a school T-shirt or sweatshirt or hat. Shouldn't the student immediately feel like part of the family? (*Boost sensory appeal*) To its credit, MIT went even further, sending its acceptance packet in a tube stuffed with a poster, refrigerator magnet, and best of all, confetti! (*Breaking the script*)
- Encourage the students to post a picture of themselves wearing the school swag on social media with a hashtag that allows them to connect with other admittees. (*Creating shared meaning*)
- Deliver the news in a personalized video from the admissions director, sent straight to the student's phone: "Katie, I just wanted to tell you how excited we are to have you join the class!" (*Deepening ties via responsiveness*) Now, obviously Ohio State can't send so many video messages, but smaller schools could, and shouldn't they exploit that advantage?
- Add anticipation by texting students that their decision will be available online at exactly 5:58 p.m., and they should use the following secret code to log in. (*Raising the stakes*)
- Have a current freshman text them the evening after they receive their admission, offering congratulations and asking whether they have any questions. (*Deepening ties via responsiveness*)
- Include a set of photos that highlight the freshman

experience: *10 Things You Should Definitely Try Your First Semester* (the library's collection of foreign films or the gym's climbing wall or the homecoming football game or the museum's archive of literary love letters . . .). (*Multiply milestones*)

That's how we imagine you using the ideas in this book. Target a specific moment and then challenge yourself: *How can I elevate it? Spark insight? Boost the sense of connection?* Life is full of "form letter in an envelope" moments, waiting to be transformed into something special.

A bit of attention and energy can transform an ordinary moment into an extraordinary one. We've seen high school graduations transformed into defining moments—not just for the graduates but for sixth graders in the audience! (*YES Prep's Signing Day*) We've seen an average hotel pool made magical by the presence of a Popsicle Hotline. We've seen the power of simple gestures: a teacher praising a student, a couple recording their fights in a journal, a pastor giving an intern the chance to preach at Easter Vigil service. And we've seen how massive changes often hinge on single moments: The Sharp staffers meet and reconnect under one roof. Stanton teachers visit parents in their homes—and really *listen* to them—for the first time. A CLTS facilitator swirls a hair in a glass of water as a crowd watches with dawning horror.

But what's the *payoff* for all these moments? Can you measure it? Does it show up on the bottom line? Yes—think of all the tangible outcomes that have been created by better moments: More revenue (Forrester data, Southwest Airlines).

Greater customer satisfaction and loyalty (Magic Castle). More motivated employees (data on recognition). More *effective* employees (purpose versus passion). And also many payoffs more personal in nature: More happiness (gratitude visits). Closer relationships (responsiveness). Self-transformation (Cinderella/ ugly duckling moments in school, stretching for insight).

Defining moments lead to countless positive and measurable outcomes, but in our judgment they are not a means to an end. They are the ends. Creating more memorable and meaningful experiences is a worthy goal—for your work, for the people you care about, and for you personally—independent of any secondary impacts. What teacher would not want to design a lesson that students still reflect on years later? What service executive would not want to create a peak experience for customers? What parents would not want to make memories for their kids that endure for decades?

Our good intentions to create these moments are often frustrated by urgent-seeming problems and pressures. School administrators harp on the upcoming state assessment, so the teacher stops planning his special lesson and teaches to the test. Some customers complain about a "pothole," so the manager shelves the peak moment she's considering and scrambles to respond.

In the short term, we prioritize fixing problems over making moments, and that choice usually feels like a smart trade-off. But over time, it backfires. Bronnie Ware, a palliative care nurse who served patients for the final weeks of their lives, wrote a moving article called "Regrets of the Dying." She shared the five most common regrets of the people she had come to know:

1. I wish I'd had the courage to live a life true to myself, not the life others expected of me. ("Most people had not honoured even a half of their dreams and had to die knowing that it was due to choices they had made, or not made.")
2. I wish I hadn't worked so hard.
3. I wish I'd had the courage to express my feelings. ("Many people suppressed their feelings in order to keep peace with others.")
4. I wish I had stayed in touch with my friends.
5. I wish that I had let myself be happier. ("Many did not realize until the end that happiness is a choice. They had stayed stuck in old patterns and habits.")

It is striking how many of the principles we've encountered would serve as antidotes to those common regrets:

1. Stretching ourselves to discover our reach;
2. Being intentional about creating peaks (or Perfect Moments, in Eugene O'Kelly's phrasing) in our personal lives;
3. Practicing courage by speaking honestly—and seeking partners who are responsive to us in the first place;
4. The value of connection (and the difficulty of creating peaks);
5. Creating moments of elevation and breaking the script to move beyond old patterns and habits.

Ware's patients were people who had let the demands of the present interfere with their hopes for the future. In life, we can work so hard to get the kinks out that we forget to put the peaks in.

2.

Finally, we'd like to share a "moment of insight" of our own that came in the course of our research. It began with a story told to us by a woman named Julie Kasten.

In 1999, Kasten said, she was sitting in her cubicle at her office in Washington, D.C., eavesdropping on the woman in the neighboring cube.

Kasten, 24, was working for a well-respected consulting firm. She had joined the firm about 18 months earlier, attracted by the chance to work in marketing communications. The cubicle next to her was reserved for the use of out-of-town executives while they were visiting the D.C. office. Kasten didn't know the woman who was using the cube that day. Nevertheless, the woman changed her life.

"She was smartly attired. . . . Blue pantsuit. Well tailored. Polished. She stuck out among the other visitors," said Kasten. "She was on the phone pretty much for the duration of her stay. And what struck me was her *enthusiasm.*

"I knew she was looking at the blank walls around her— same as mine. But she was so skillful at what she was doing, and obviously enjoying herself."

It occurred to Kasten that the woman was doing the same job she would be doing someday if she advanced at the firm.

Kasten's next thoughts came as a jolt.

If that's what success in this role sounds like, I don't want it. She's energized by what she's talking about. But it bores me to death.

"I imagined myself wanting to be like she was," Kasten said. "But talking about something else."

At that moment, she knew she would quit her job.

Kasten began plotting her exit. A few months later, she visited a career counselor, hoping to discover a job that better suited her interests. That's when her life shifted a second time.

The counselor listened to her aspirations and offered some tools—personality tests and skills assessments—to clarify the kind of work she wanted to do. Armed with this data, the counselor suggested a few careers that might fit her. But Kasten had already decided. She remembers looking at the counselor, thinking, *I want to do what you do.*

A few months later, in the fall of 1999, Kasten was enrolled in graduate school for counseling. As of 2016, she had been a career counselor for 14 years.

Two lightning-bolt moments changed Kasten's career. Neither one was foreseen. They just happened, she acted, and in an instant, her life was different.

Kasten's experience was a classic "crystallization of discontent" moment, as we described in Chapter 5. We were struck by the suddenness of her realizations, and we were interested in collecting other crystallizing moments. So we sent Kasten's story to our newsletter subscribers, asking if anyone had experienced something similar. Our question struck a nerve. We received more than 400 replies, many of them achingly personal—stories of marriages collapsing and love reborn, stories of careers abandoned and embraced.* Here's a sampling:

- Suresh Mistry was working as an assistant manager at Lloyds Bank in London. Every day he sat at his desk with an "out of order" report that listed all the business clients who had breached their overdraft or loan limits. He had to decide whether to bounce their checks or let them slide. Opposite him was his manager, who was also sitting with an "out of order" report. "The only difference was that the numbers on his list had an extra 0," Mistry wrote. "I dealt in £10,000s. He dealt in £100,0000s. It was then that I spotted the Divisional Director in his glass office in the corner. He sat behind a large desk with a sheet of paper in front of him. Yup, you've guessed it—an out of order list with £1,000,000s. I saw my future laid out in front of me and I despaired." Within a week, Mistry had applied for a new job in sales and marketing, a field he has enjoyed for more than 20 years now.

---

* Lest you think we have an army of enthusiastic readers who respond to our every query, let us refer you to a previous newsletter where we asked for decision-making stories and received exactly two responses, one of which was Dan's anxious test to see if the survey tool was functioning properly.

- Warren Talbot and his wife, Betsy—both 37—were having dinner with friends in a Seattle restaurant. Someone asked, "What would you do if you knew you would not live until 40?" Warren and his wife turned to each other, and without having discussed it, said, "We'd travel the world." The question was not idle chatter for them—the Talbots had a close friend who was in the hospital after suffering a brain aneurysm. They were aware how short life can be. The next morning, they set a date two years into the future—October 1, 2010—to begin their world travel. During those two years, they planned and saved, sold everything they owned, and then left Seattle on exactly the date they had set. Their first stop: a rammed-earth house in northern Ecuador. "We travelled full time for 3+ years," the Talbots wrote us, "and now own a home in the hills of southern Spain which we use as a base and continue to explore. We're both 45 now and there is not a moment we've regretted the choice we made that night 8 years ago."
- Nancy Schaufele was in her late 20s, a housewife with two young children. Her husband had just been diagnosed with cancer. One morning she was sitting on her porch, sipping coffee, preparing for the day ahead. "And then it hit me," she wrote. "I was possibly going to have to raise two children alone. Really alone. No skills, no education and no husband. It was an OMG moment. A lightning bolt from the sky." She resolved to go back to school, to learn the skills

she'd need to launch a career. But when she went to register, she said, "my legs were like rubber." She was anxious, intimidated. She made it to the administration building, burst into tears, turned around, and went home. "When I got home and walked in the door, the first thing I saw was my 2 year old daughter playing with her dad. I remember asking myself that hard question: 'How I could ever encourage my daughter to be "more" if I couldn't even register for one college course?' I turned around and went back to the school." She finished college and graduate school, started a business, sold it, and now advises female business owners and entrepreneurs.

When we began to read these powerful stories, we thought we were reading about epiphanies. "Eureka!" moments. But what dawned on us, as we read more of them, is that these were not stories about sudden realizations. These were stories about *action*.

Julie Kasten visited a career counselor. Suresh Mistry applied for a new job. Warren Talbot and his wife set a date to travel the world. Nancy Schaufele turned around and went back to register for college.

Often, what looks like a moment of serendipity is actually a moment of intentionality. What Kasten, Mistry, and the others experienced as the shock of an insight was actually, we came to believe, the whiplash caused by *realizing they could ACT* and then willfully jolting their lives in a new direction. They were not *receiving* a moment, they were *seizing* it.

And that's a critical distinction. Some defining moments are orchestrated. But many other moments we've encountered are *plunged into:* Some hotel staffers discover a little boy has left behind his stuffed giraffe and decide to do something special for him. A man decides to push past small talk with his coworker and realizes how much they have in common. A mentor chooses to stay all night with his psychiatric intern who has witnessed a tragedy.

This is what we hope you take away from this book: Stay alert to the promise that moments hold. These moments do not need to be "produced." Yes, we examined some moments that took a lot of time and money to plan: The Sharp All-Staff Assembly. Signing Day. The Trial of Human Nature. And, yes, it often takes real effort to elevate a moment properly—it matters that the Trial was held in a courtroom and not in the school cafeteria. But keep in mind these are once-a-year events!

Many of the moments in this book, though, are free and unproduced—the kinds of moments that arise every day. You compliment a colleague on the way she handled a client emergency. (*Recognize others*) You ask your children at the dinner table, "What have you failed at this week?" (*Stretch for insight*) You and a colleague decide to meet after work for a cupcake. (*Break the script*)

The most precious moments are often the ones that cost the least. In June 2007, Darcy Daniel's three-year-old daughter, Wendy, came down with a stomachache. A doctor in the rural Vermont town where they lived discovered she had a severe *E. coli* infection, which triggered an escalating progression of health threats: Her kidneys failed and she spent weeks on dialysis. Horrible stomachaches led to a portion of her colon being removed, twice. Infections from the repeated surgeries led to heart failure; she coded and had to be resuscitated. She desperately needed a kidney transplant, but none of the many people who volunteered were compatible.

She spent Halloween in the hospital; her costume was laid on top of her, because she had too many tubes coming out of her body to put it on. Thanksgiving came and went. One day in December, not long before Christmas, it began to snow outside. For a child from Vermont, it was cruel, having to watch the snow through the windows. Wendy loved to make snowmen, to go sleigh riding. She hadn't been outside for two months.

Her lead nurse, Cori Fogarty, and patient care associate Jessica Marsh hatched a plan. If Wendy couldn't play in the snow, they would bring the snow to her. But it was more complicated than that. Because of Wendy's heart condition, the staff was monitoring every milliliter of water that she consumed. So Jessica went and filled an emesis bucket with snow, weighed it, let it melt, and then poured it into a graduated cylinder. Now they knew how to translate the weight of snow into its volume of water. So they went and refilled the bucket with exactly the right amount of snow so that if Wendy ate it all—as three-year-olds are prone to do—she'd be just fine.

When they brought the bowl of snow into Wendy's room, she lit up. "I have never seen such joy and pure innocence on a child's face," said Marsh.

"Can you imagine," said Darcy, "a child who has only seen the inside of a hospital room for months, who only knew the sounds of the machines and the buzzers, the television, the whoosh of the forced air, who only knew the sterility of the meal trays, the plastic covered hospital bed, the stethoscope hanging over her head, getting a bowl of snow? . . . It was bliss, it was joy. She thought it was the best thing in the world. . . . It reminded her of home."

Wendy's long nightmare eventually ended. She received a successful kidney transplant and, since then, has grown into a healthy young girl. She plays soccer, runs triathlons, and won medals in the Transplant Olympics. Mercifully, she has forgotten much of her health ordeal. But her mom hasn't.

Darcy wrote in a blog post years later about the bucket of snow: "It is those moments of compassion and spontancity that we are grateful for, now, looking back. It's easy to forget the monotony of the endless days that stretched together during her recovery. But that one moment of brightness, that is one moment that we will never forget."

That's what a defining moment looks like. A burst of magic—thoughtful, playful, emotional—that was conjured into reality by two caregivers who thought a sick girl deserved an escape.

And that's the charge for all of us: to defy the forgettable flatness of everyday work and life by creating a few precious moments.

What if every organization in the world offered new employees an unforgettable first-day experience?

What if every student had an academic experience as memorable as prom?

What if every patient was asked, "What matters to you?"

What if you called that old friend right now and finally made that road trip happen?

What if we didn't just *remember* the defining moments of our lives but *made* them?

We can be the designers of moments that deliver elevation and insight and pride and connection. These extraordinary minutes and hours and days—they are what make life meaningful. And they are ours to create.

Want More?

If you've finished *The Power of Moments* and are hungry for more, visit our website: http://www.thepowerofmoments.com. When you sign up for our newsletter, you get instant access to *free* materials like these:

- **1-Page Overview**. A printable overview of the Elevation-Insight-Pride-Connection framework, perfect for tacking up next to your desk.
- **The Book Club Guide**. If you're reading *The Power of Moments* as part of a book club, this guide offers suggested questions and topics to guide your discussion.
- **Recommended Reading List**. All of our sources are available to you in the endnotes in this book, of course.

But in this list we share the eight books and articles that we found most fascinating or useful.

- **The Power of Moments for Friends and Family**. An inspiring and wide-ranging set of examples showing how to share more special moments with the people closest to you. It includes: birthday and anniversary ideas, more Art Aron–style questions, actual examples of the "Saturday Surprise" (see Chapter 4), traditions from other cultures that we should embrace, and more.
- **The Power of Moments podcasts**. Short podcasts, recorded by the authors, that cover the following topics in more depth:
  - *Defining moments in education*
  - *Defining moments in health care*
  - *Defining moments in customer experiences*
  - *Defining moments for employees*

Appendix

Dealing with Moments of Trauma

We're sorry that you're here. Whatever you're facing, know that there are other people who have walked in your shoes, and their experiences can give you reasons to hope even in the midst of trauma.

Moments of trauma cause profound pain and hardship; what's less intuitive is that they also, in some cases, produce positive growth, a phenomenon called "posttraumatic growth." This growth does not make the tragedy less tragic, and it does not cure the underlying pain. But the researchers Richard Tedeschi and Lawrence Calhoun have found that "great good can come from great suffering."

Post-traumatic growth has been documented among people who have lost a spouse; veterans of combat; refugees forced to flee their home country; patients with HIV or cancer; parents with very sick children; and people who have been sexually assaulted or abused. Some studies have found that trauma survivors report positive personal changes at a *higher* level than people who have not experienced trauma.

What follows are five recommendations for finding great good in great suffering. The recommendations are inspired by the five domains where trauma survivors regularly report positive growth. (These five domains are drawn from the work of the post-traumatic growth researchers Tedeschi and Calhoun. This appendix draws heavily on a particular review article of theirs—see the citation at the end of the Appendix. All quotations come from the review article.)

Look for small peaks. People who have experienced trauma often report that they have a greater capacity to enjoy small things in life that previously they might have ignored: a beautiful garden, a strong cup of coffee, a morning with a child. Hamilton Jordan, former presidential advisor to Bill Clinton, said,

> *After my first cancer, even the smallest joys in life took on a special meaning—watching a beautiful sunset, a hug from my child, a laugh with [wife] Dorothy. That feeling has not diminished with time. After my second and third cancers, the simple joys of life are everywhere and are boundless, as I cherish my family and friends and contemplate the rest of my life, a life I certainly do not take for granted.*

Geology professor Sally Walker, who survived an airline crash that killed 83 others, said, "When I got home, the sky was brighter, I paid attention to the texture of sidewalks. It was like being in a movie. . . . [Now] Everything is a gift."

In Chapter 3, we tell the story of Eugene O'Kelly, who was diagnosed with terminal brain cancer and told he had three months to live. In response, he began to create a series of "Perfect Moments" he could share with loved ones—for instance, enjoying a nice meal and strolling afterward through Central Park. He marveled how these special moments allowed him to live "a month in a week."

Celebrate and honor relationships. One parent, describing the death of her son, said, "When he died people just came out of the woodwork" to help. She experienced renewed appreciation for her friends. She came to cherish her husband more.

Not all friends are active in reaching out. Many trauma sufferers have noted that in tough times you find out who your real friends are. By winnowing unsupportive relationships and rededicating themselves to the supportive ones, people often emerge feeling more secure and cared for. They also find that they have acquired a heightened sense of compassion and empathy for others who are grieving or in pain.

In Chapter 11, we discuss ways to create closer relationships, including the idea of "responsiveness," which says that relationships grow when partners understand, validate, and care for each other. As a trauma survivor, you are in a good position to be responsive to others—you can understand what other trauma sufferers are going through, and you are in a position to validate their thoughts and reactions because you have grappled with tragedy. You can provide loving support in ways that might be more challenging for others. For example, many parents who have lost a child find that their friends eventually stop mentioning the child, fearing that the mention might trigger painful memories. But parents who have lost a child know that the child is never far from mind. So making a comment like "Mark would have loved this vacation/football game/new car" is more likely to be received as thoughtful and warm rather than as reopening an old wound.

Acknowledge your strength. A bereaved parent said, "I can handle things better. Things that used to be big deals just aren't big deals anymore." People use the trauma as a test of their capacity to stretch, endure hardship, and persevere. Many said, "If I can handle this then I can handle just about anything."

In Chapter 6, we share the story of a young psychiatrist, Michael Dinneen, who blamed himself for the suicide of a patient that happened on his watch. His mentor stayed with him through the night, helping him to see that he could endure the pain and self-doubt. As a result of the experience, Dinneen was motivated to become a mentor himself—for decades, he has been a source of strength to others, showing them that they can overcome hardship.

Identify new possibilities. Individuals who are enduring trauma sometimes find themselves identifying new possibilities for their lives: new work, new passions, new paths.

A study by Elaine Wethington, a medical sociologist at Cornell, found that a third of people who were laid off characterized the event as having a positive impact on their lives. And almost 45% of people who had a serious illness said the same! This is not to deny the experience of the two-thirds of people who said being laid off had a negative impact. But some people find that when one door closes, another opens.

Look for spiritual insight. Many trauma survivors find comfort in spiritual practice during their struggle. One person said, "I believe that God got me through it. Five or six years ago I didn't have those beliefs. And I don't know what I would do without Him now." The researchers Tedeschi and Calhoun observe that even nonreligious people can experience "greater engagement with fundamental existential questions and that engagement in itself may be experienced as growth."

None of the discussion above is intended to imply that dealing with trauma is simple, or that your own "growth" should be the focus of your energies. A quote from Rabbi Harold Kushner, who lost a child, captures what it means to welcome growth while wishing it had never happened:

> *I am a more sensitive person, a more effective pastor, a more sympathetic counselor because of Aaron's life and death than I would ever have been without it. And I would give up all of those gains in a second if I could have my son back. If I could choose, I would forego all of the spiritual growth and depth which has come my way because of our experiences. . . . But I cannot choose.*

Other Recommended Reading

For more on the academic research from which this appendix is drawn, see: Richard G. Tedeschi and Lawrence G. Calhoun (2004). "Posttraumatic Growth: Conceptual Foundations and

Empirical Evidence," *Psychological Inquiry* 15: 1–18. The researchers have a test of post-traumatic growth, called the Post-traumatic Growth Inventory (PTGI), that you can find online. We also recommend the excellent *Option B: Facing Adversity, Building Resilience, and Finding Joy* by Adam Grant and Sheryl Sandberg. Also see:

- Jane McGonigal (2015). *SuperBetter: The Power of Living Gamefully*. New York: Penguin.

- James Pennebaker and John Evans (2014). *Expressive Writing: Words That Heal*. Enumclaw, WA: Idyll Arbor.

Acknowledgments

We are deeply grateful to the readers who contributed feedback on early drafts of this book. It is no small commitment that we asked of you—spending hours reading a half-baked book and sharing with us what was working and what wasn't. Your comments led to some big changes and countless small ones, all positive (including saving other readers from many unfunny jokes). Thanks, too, to the people who joined us for group discussions in Washington, D.C., Atlanta, and New York City. The book got so much better thanks to your ideas—we hope you can tell.

A heartfelt thanks to those who pointed us toward ideas or stories that made it into the book: to Joe McCannon for highlighting the idea of "shared struggle"; to Nella Garcia and Mark DiBella for sharing the Signing Day story; to Cheryl Fergerson, Addie Simmons, and Victor Mata for sharing some of their time on Senior Signing Day 2016; to Angela Duckworth and Lauren Eskreis-Winkler for inspirations and research pointers; to Fred Houston for sharing the Deloitte retirement tradition. To Patricia Dinneen for the connection to Michael Palmer; to Robert Heuermann for the "inanimate carbon rod" pointer; to William Fultz for the treasure chest idea; to Matt Dixon for discussion of the offense/defense idea in Chapter 3; to Rabbi Naphtali Lavenda for sharing the story of rabbinical role-play; to Megan Burns for encouraging us to dig into the Forrester data and to Laura Tramm and Roxana Strohmenger for helping us with the analysis; to Frank Tooley, Katie Boynton, and Mike Overly for helping us solve the flight safety announcement mystery—and for doing battle with the Southwest bureaucracy (hello legal department!) to get us permission to tell the story; and to Eli Finkel for his eagle-eyed identification of "responsiveness" as the critical ingredient missing from our initial writing about connection.

There were also several people who helped us along the way through multiple conversations on many different aspects of defining moments. Thanks to Soon Yu, Paul Maloney, Darren Ross, Nick Stroud, Bridget Stalkamp, and Megan Burns.

Thanks to Lorna Lippes and Maya Valluru for research assistance (and especially for slogging through hundreds of online reviews of service experiences). Extra-special notes of appreciation to Christy Darnell for managing our reader feedback, and to Dave Vance for his comedic inspirations, and to Peter Griffin for his editing magic.

We feel so lucky to have partners like Christy Fletcher and

her crew at Fletcher & Company, as well as our new team at Simon & Schuster, where we have reunited with our first editor, Ben Loehnen. Ben, thank you for giving us our first shot in this business—and now our fourth.

None of our work would be possible without the love and support of our (highly responsive!) family. We love you, Mom, Dad, Susan, Susan Joy, Emory, Aubrey, Amanda, Josephine, Oksana, Hunter, and Darby.

Notes

Chapter 1: Defining Moments

1 **YES Prep Signing Day.** This story draws on Dan's interviews with Donald Kamentz in February 2015 and Chris Barbic in May 2016 and email exchanges with both. Also Dan's interview with Mayra Valle in July 2016 and attendance at May 2016 Signing Day in Houston.

7 **Buckets filled with frigid 57-degree water.** Ice bucket study, peak-end concept, and duration neglect from D. Kahneman, B. L. Fredrickson, C. A. Schreiber, and D. A. Redelmeier (1993). "When More Pain Is Preferred to Less: Adding a Better End," *Psychological Science* 4: 401–5.

9 **Remember flagship moments: the peaks, the pits, and the transitions.** Daniel Kahneman, the psychologist who won the Nobel Prize in Economics, began this work with a flurry of interesting papers in the 1990s, including papers on how people experience the consumption of short film clips and how patients experience colonoscopies.

Research consistently confirms the importance of extreme moments (peaks and pits). As Carey Morewedge notes in a review of the field of predicted utility, when baseball fans are asked to recall a baseball game, they typically recall the most fantastic game they can remember. When colonoscopy patients are asked to recall a procedure, they place heavy weight on the most painful moment. When vacationers on a three-week cycling vacation in California are asked to recall the ride, they tend to focus on the best moments.

As we suggest in the first chapter, we believe it's more useful to think in terms of "peaks and transitions" than "peaks and ends." One reason is the blurriness between endings and beginnings that we alluded to. Another is the abundant research on the importance of beginnings. We mention that 40% of college memories come from September; another data point is that the first six weeks of the freshman year generate more long-term memories than the entire junior year (which suggests an immediate way of cutting college expenses).

More generally, there is evidence that information that comes at the beginning of an experience receives more attention and weight. Memories tend to show primacy effects (greater memory for things at the beginning of a sequence) and recency effects (greater memory at the end). Work on perceptions of others show that information early in interaction is over-weighted.

For a good summary of the research that has been done on predicted utility, see Carey K. Morewedge (2015), "Utility: Anticipated, Experienced, and Remembered," in Gideon Keren and George Wu, eds., *The Wiley Black-well Handbook of Judgement and Decision Making,* pp. 295–30. Malden, MA: Wiley.

The colonoscopy study is Daniel Kahneman and Donald A. Redelmeier (1996). "Patients' Memories of Painful Medical Treatments: Real-time and Retrospective Evaluations of Two Minimally Invasive Procedures," *Pain* 66(1): 3–8. The cold water task is in Daniel Kahneman, Barbara L. Fredrickson, Charles A. Schreiber, and Donald A. Redelmeier (1993). "When More Pain Is Preferred to Less: Adding a Better End," *Psychological Science,* 4(6): 401–5. The research on memories for college events is summarized in David B. Pillemer (2000). *Momentous Events, Vivid Memories: How Unforgettable Moments Help Us Understand the Meaning of Our Lives.* Cambridge, MA: Harvard University Press. The importance of September in college memories is from p. 126.

9 **Magic Castle Hotel.** Description of Magic Castle from in-person visits by Chip and Dan and conversations between Chip and Darren Ross, chief operating officer and general manager, at Magic Castle Hotel LLC. Review stats consulted on January 20, 2017: https://www.tripadvisor.com/Hotel _Review-g32655-d84502-Reviews-Magic_Castle_Hotel-Los_Angeles _California.html.

Chapter 2: Thinking in Moments

19 **Gloves filled with angry, stinging, bullet ants.** https://www.globalcitizen.org/en/content/13-amazing-coming-of-age-traditions-from-around-th/.

20 **John Deere First Day Experience.** Story from Dan's interviews with Lani Lorenz Fry, January 2016 (and subsequent email exchanges); Lewis Carbone, December 2015; and Mukul Varshney (India office), January 2016.

22 **"Reverse wedding" story from Kenneth Doka.** From Dan's interview with Doka in January 2016.

24 **New Year's resolutions/"fresh start" theory.** The Katherine Milkman quote is from an interview with Stephen Dubner on the Freakonomics podcast, http://freakonomics.com/2015/03/13/when-willpower-isnt-enough-full-transcript/. The fitness center data is in Hengchen Dai, Katherine L. Milkman, and Jason Riis (2014). "The Fresh Start Effect: Temporal Landmarks Motivate Aspirational Behavior," *Management Science* 60(10): 2563–82, http://dx.doi.org/10.1287/mnsc.2014.1901.

25 **Most significant birthdays.** Adam L. Alter and Hal E. Hershfield (2014). "People Search for Meaning When They Approach a New Decade in Chronological Age," *PNAS* 111, http://www.pnas.org/content/111/48/17066.

27 **Fitbit badges.** From author experience (Dan's). Chip is still trying to accumulate enough miles for his Koala Badge. For more examples of Fitbit badges, see http://www.developgoodhabits.com/fitbit-badge-list/.

28   **Car leases.** Eric A. Taub (2016, October 27). "Let the Lessee Beware: Car Leases Can Be the Most Binding of Contracts," *New York Times,* https://www.nytimes.com/2016/10/28/automobiles/let-the-lessee-beware-car-leases-can-be-the-most-binding-of-contracts.html.

28   **Intermountain Healthcare.** Leonard L. Berry, Scott W. Davis, and Jody Wilmet (2015, October). "When the Customer Is Stressed," *Harvard Business Review.*

29   **25% of positive encounters started as service failures.** Mary Jo Bitner, Bernard H. Booms, and Mary Stanfield Tetreault (1990). "The Service Encounter: Diagnosing Favorable and Unfavorable Incidents," *Journal of Marketing* 54: 71–84.

29   **Doug Dietz MRI Adventure series.** Dietz MRI story from his TED talk, https://www.youtube.com/watch?v=jajduxPD6H4, plus Dan's interview with Dietz in July 2016. The quote about taking 1 minute to get kids on the table, versus 10, came from the interview, as did the quote about Bobby and the cable car. The other quotes come from the TED Talk. Some descriptions drawn from documents shared by Dietz. The 80% statistic, and the drop in need for sedation at Children's Hospital, is from http://www.jsonline.com/business/by-turning-medical-scans-into-adventures-ge-eases-childrens-fears-b99647870z1-366161191.html.

34   **Transition to middle school/locker races.** From Chip's communication with Michael Reimer, October 2016.

35   **Mac OS 9 eulogy.** Transcribed from https://www.youtube.com/watch?v=2Ya2nY12y3Q.

35   **Deloitte retirement.** Dan attended one of these in June 2016 in Washington, D.C.

Chapter 3: Build Peaks

47   **Hillsdale High, Trial of Human Nature.** This story is drawn from Dan's interviews and subsequent email exchanges in January 2016 with Greg Jouriles, Susan Bedford, Jeff Gilbert, and Greg Lance, as well as documents shared by them, plus a transcript of Greg Lance's appearance in Chip's class in November 2009. Chip and Dan also attended the Trial in December 2016.

53   **35,000 high schools.** http://www2.ed.gov/about/offices/list/ovae/pi/hs/hsfacts.html.

55   **Tracked down the cocktail recipe.** From Chip's interview with Darren Ross in June 2015.

55   **One exception to this logic.** Matthew Dixon, Nick Toman, and Rick Delisi wrote a smart and practical book called *The Effortless Experience,* which reports on the results of a study of 97,000 customer-support interactions via phone or Web. (Dan wrote the book's foreword.) The authors found that "there is virtually no difference at all between the loyalty of those customers whose expectations are exceeded and those whose expectations are simply met." They add that "companies tend to grossly underestimate the benefit of simply meeting customer expectations." In other words, if a customer is calling about a problem with his credit card or cable service, then he just wants it fixed, quickly. He doesn't want to be "delighted." It's plenty delightful to resolve the issue without transferring him or making him repeat himself. This is a situation where being "mostly forgettable" is a good thing. So, if your job involves resolving customer issues remotely (via phone or Web), forget about building peaks. Instead, focus on filling pits—those delays or handoffs that irritate the customer. And to learn practical ways to fill those pits, read the book! Matthew Dixon, Nick Toman, and Rick Delisi (2013). *The Effortless Experience*. New York: Portfolio.

55   **"To exceed customer expectations."** From Dan's call with Len Berry, August 2016.

56   **Customer experience, Plan A/ Plan B.** The customer experience survey is described in Rick Parrish with Harley Manning, Roxana Strohmenger, Gabriella Zoia, and Rachel Birrell (2016). "The US Customer Experience Index," 2016, Forrester. CX Index is a trademark of Forrester Research, Inc.

60   **We obsess about problems and negative information.** R. F. Baumeister, E. Bratslavsky, C. Finkenauer, and K. D. Vohs (2001). "Bad Is Stronger than Good," *Review of General Psychology* 5: 323–70.

62   **Footnote on wedding expenses.** Andrew M. Francis and Hugo M. Mialon (2014). "'A Diamond Is Forever' and Other Fairy Tales: The Relationship Between Wedding Expenses and Marriage Duration," Social Science Research Network, https://papers.ssrn.com/sol3/papers2.cfm?abstract

_id=2501480. In later chapters, we will discuss "moments of connection." These researchers also found that having more people at a wedding led to reduced likelihood of breakup.

65   Eugene O'Kelly, *Chasing Daylight.* Eugene O'Kelly and Andrew Postman (2005). *Chasing Daylight: How My Forthcoming Death Transformed My Life.* New York: McGraw-Hill.

Chapter 4: Break the Script

69   **Joshie the giraffe at the Ritz.** Joshie story from http://www.huffington post.com/chris-hurn/stuffed-giraffe-shows-wha_b_1524038.html.

71   **Concept of a script.** The hamburger and birthday party examples are from a book by two psychologists who did the most to study the impact of scripts: Roger C. Schank and Robert P. Abelson (1977). *Scripts, Plans, and Knowledge.* Hillsdale, NJ: Lawrence Erlbaum.

72   **Strategic surprise/"Well-aimed surprise."** We considered a related point in our book *Made to Stick,* which explains how to make communication stickier. *Made to Stick* discussed the difference between "gimmicky surprise" and "core surprise" in the context of making messages unexpected. A core surprise is one that helps attract attention to the key message being expressed (as opposed to a cheap joke or stunt that earns attention but is irrelevant). Similarly, in this chapter, we are recommending "strategic surprise," which is generated by breaking a known script in a way that reinforces your goals (as with the Ritz story).

72   **"Delightful surprises."** Stat from John C. Crotts and Vincent P. Magnini (2011). "The Customer Delight Construct: Is Surprise Essential?" *Annals of Tourism Research* 38(2): 719–22. Cited in Tania Luna and LeeAnn Renninger (2015). *Surprise: Embrace the Unpredictable and Engineer the Unexpected.* New York: Penguin Books, p. 137.

73   **Pret A Manger.** The "smile on my face" quote is from Matt Watkinson (2013). *The Ten Principles Behind Great Customer Experiences.* Harlow, England: Pearson, p. 107. The other quotes are from http://www.standard .co.uk/news/london/pret-a-manger-staff-give-free-coffee-to-their-favou rite-customers-sandwich-chain-boss-reveals-10191611.html.

74   **Southwest Airlines flight safety announcements.** The flight safety jokes are on cloud-shaped plaques on a wall at Southwest corporate head-quarters in Dallas, close to the cafeteria. The list price of a Boeing 737-800 is $72 million but airlines don't pay list. The actual prices they do pay are highly secret but occasionally word leaks out about one deal or another; a blogger cited a few recent examples buried in airline's financial statements and the going price looks to be $50 million or so: http://blog.seattlepi.com /aerospace/2009/07/01/how-much-is-a-shiny-new-boeing-737-worth-not-72-million/. Chip did a workshop for Southwest in July 2016. The statistics in the analysis of the flight safety announcements are from Frank Tooley, Katie Boynton, and Mike Overly between August 2016 and January 2017.

76   **Serial entrepreneur Scott Beck.** From Dan's interview with Scott Beck, October 2015.

78   **Examples of Saturday Surprise.** Various survey responses, March 2016.

78   **VF Corporation meeting, "going outside."** The details about the meet-ings come from Chip's interviews with Stephen Dull in July 2016, and with Soon Yu in July, August, and December 2016. Full disclosure: Chip was invited to deliver several paid speeches and workshops at VF Corporation, which is how he met Soon Yu and learned about this story. The JanSport backpack story is told in an internal "Bright Spot" video. (Consistent with the recommendations in our book *Switch*, VF made an effort to advertise bright spot situations where the change was already happening—where people had produced some clear wins from going outside.)

83   **$1.6 billion in value.** Estimate from Dull, made by rolling up the projec-tions of each of the project owners who had to justify their business impact to VF corporate leaders. Projections are often wildly optimistic so Dull, Yu, and their team went with a conservative approach of counting only the predicted first three years' revenue for most products. The sum added up to more than $1.6 billion. They also tracked the revenues from ideas that had already reached the market, and at press time, VF had brought to market about one-third of the $1.6 billion potential revenue portfolio.

83   **The Reminiscence Bump.** Dorthe Berntsen and David M. Rubin (2004). "Cultural Life Scripts Structure Recall from Autobiographical Memory," *Memory & Cognition* 32(3): 427–42. The Hammond quote is from Claudia

Hammond (2012). *Time Warped: Unlocking the Mysteries of Time Perception.* Toronto: House of Anansi Press.

85 **The oddball effect is from a study by Vani Pariyadath and David Eagleman (2007).** "The Effect of Predictability on Subjective Duration," *PLoS ONE* 2(11), http://journals.plos.org/plosone/article?id=10.1371/journal.pone.0001264. Eagleman explains the oddball effect as arising from boredom in this blog entry: http://blogs.nature.com/news/2011/11/on_stretching_time.html.

85 **150-foot free fall.** Study description and result from Bulkhard Bilger, "The Possibilian," *New Yorker,* April 25, 2011.

86 **"We feel most alive" when things are not certain.** Found in the introduction to Luna and Renninger, *Surprise,* p. xx.

89 **Clinic 2: Refresh a Meeting.** This scenario is based on a conversation between Rev. Frey and Dan in July 2016.

Chapter 5: Trip Over the Truth

97 *BMJ* most important medical milestones. Sarah Boseley (2007, January 19). "Sanitation Rated the Greatest Medical Advance in 150 Years," http://www.theguardian.com/society/2007/jan/19/health.medicineandhealth3.

97 **About a billion people.** World Health Organization, http://www.who.int/water_sanitation_health/mdg1/en/.

99 **"Even better than my house."** "Shit Matters," video, https://www.youtube.com/watch?v=_NSwL1TCaoY#t=11.

99 **60 countries around the world.** From CLTS home page, http://www.cltsfoundation.org/.

99 **A CLTS facilitator arrives.** Most of the description of the transect walk is from the CLTS handbook, which can be downloaded at the link below, with some additional color from an interview between Dan and Kar in January 2016. Kamal Kar (2008). *Handbook on Community-Led Total Sanitation.* http://www.communityledtotalsanitation.org/sites/communityledtotalsanitation.org/files/cltshandbook.pdf.

102 **Declined from 34% to 1%.** The decline in open defecation is from CLTS annual report, 2014–15, and CLTS report "Igniting Action/Asia."

102 **"The naked truth is out."** Quote from Dan's interview with Kar.

104 **Scott Guthrie, Microsoft Azure.** Story from http://fortune.com/micro soft-fortune-500-cloud-computing/.

106 **Course Design Institute.** Dan interviewed Michael Palmer in June 2015 and attended the CDI in July 2015. The teacher quotes are from that workshop. Dan also interviewed Christ (January 2016) and Lawrence (August 2015). The course evaluation data and the "exponentially improved" quote are from http://cte.virginia.edu/programs/course-design-institute/testi monials/.

Chapter 6: Stretch for Insight

113 **Lea Chadwell opens a bakery.** Dan interviewed Chadwell in July 2016. Thanks to Brian Kurth of PivotPlanet for the introduction.

116 **Benefits of self-insight.** Rick Harrington and Donald A. Loffredo (2011). "Insight, Rumination, and Self-Reflection as Predictors of Well-Being," *Journal of Psychology* 145(1). A thank-you to Tasha Eurich for inspiring us to check out this literature. If you find this interesting you should look up Tasha's book on self-insight (2017), *Insight: Why We're Not as Self-Aware as We Think, and How Seeing Ourselves Clearly Helps Us Succeed at Work and in Life.* New York: Crown Business.

116 **Study abroad in Rome.** Response to a survey conducted by authors in December 2015

117 *Reflecting* or *ruminating.* See Chapters 5 and 6 of Tasha Eurich's book *Insight* (citation above).

117 **Action leads to insight.** We were impressed with ourselves when we came up with this snappy action/insight quote but some cursory googling showed us that Steve Chalke was saying it nine years ago.

118 **Michael Dinneen patient suicide.** Dan interviewed Dineen about this story in June 2015, and Ridenour in June 2016

121 **Honig Easter Sunday sermon.** Honig contributed this story in March 2016 and we followed up in an email exchange in January 2017.

122 **High standards + assurance.** The research study is in David Scott Yeager et al. (2014). "Breaking the Cycle of Mistrust: Wise Interventions to Provide

Critical Feedback Across the Racial Divide," *Journal of Experimental Psychology* 143(2): 804–24.

123 **Six Sigma black belt.** This story was originally surfaced in a survey response submitted by Dale Phelps in March 2016 and subsequent interviews by Dan with Phelps and Ranjani Sreenivasan in August 2016.

127 **Blakely, Spanx.** Most of the Blakely story, including most of her quotes, are pulled from her chapter in Gillian Zoe Segal (2015). *Getting There: A Book of Mentors.* New York: Abrams Image. The timeline of events in the case study is drawn from http://www.spanx.com/years-of-great-rears. The "grew immune to the word 'no'" quote is from a talk Blakely gave to *Inc.* magazine's Women's Summit in March 2016. It is both insightful and funny. http://www.inc.com/sara-blakely/how-spanx-founder-turned-5000-dollars-into-a-billion-dollar-undergarment-business.html.

134 **Clinic 3: Panda Garden House.** This name was inspired by a *Washington Post* piece that analyzed the names of almost every Chinese restaurant in the country. As the authors wrote, "Americans have been trained to expect Chinese food at places with names like 'Golden Dragon Buffet.' If you were to open a Chinese restaurant named like 'Dorchester Meadows' it would probably tank." From Roberto A. Ferdman and Christopher Ingraham (2016, April 8), "We Analyzed the Names of Almost Every Chinese Restaurant in America. This Is What We Learned," Wonkblog, https://www.washingtonpost.com/news/wonk/wp/2016/04/08/we-analyzed-the-names-of-almost-every-chinese-restaurant-in-america-this-is-what-we-learned/?utm_term=.e32614cde10a.

Chapter 7: Recognize Others

141 **Kira Sloop, singer.** The story is from interviews by Dan with Sloop in August 2015 and January 2016.

144 **Cinderellas and ugly ducklings.** Gad Yair (2009). "Cinderellas and Ugly Ducklings: Positive Turning Points in Students' Educational Careers—Exploratory Evidence and a Future Agenda," *British Educational Research Journal* 35(3): 351–70.

145 **Four similar studies of workplace motivation.** Carolyn Wiley (1997).

"What Motivates Employees According to Over 40 Years of Motivation Surveys," *International Journal of Manpower* 18(3): 263–80.

146 **Top reason people leave jobs.** Bob Nelson (1997). *1501 Ways to Reward Employees.* New York: Workman.

147 **Recognition experts have advice.** Advice from Luthans Stajkovic (2009). "Provide Recognition for Performance Improvement." In *Handbook of Principles of Organizational Behavior.* West Sussex: Wiley, pp. 239–52.

147 **Prepping the backroom/Noticed an error.** The two quotes here came from a set of people who signed up on Amazon's MTurk to participate in research studies.

148 **Keith Risinger, Bose headset.** Risinger story from interviews with Chip and Risinger in January 2016 and October 2014, and Dan and Risinger in January 2016. Dan interviewed Hughes in January 2016. Interesting fact about Hughes: He is a professional softball player. A Hall of Famer, in fact. His professional status means he's banned from playing softball for recreation leagues, so don't get any ideas for your office team.

151 **DonorsChoose.** Dan interviewed Ahmad and Pace in July 2016, and Julie Prieto in May 2016 and September 2016. Barbara Cvenic provided information in October 2016 about the positive effect of thank-yous on subsequent donations. Thanks also to Missy Sherburne and Cesar Bocanegra for additional color.

153 **Roughly a million thank-yous.** Julia Prieto email August 2016: "Our fiscal year just wrapped with our total Per outgoing number at 90,422. That total multiplied by the average number of thank-yous in each envelope (11) puts us right at 994,642."

155 **Seligman letter of gratitude exercise.** This version of the exercise is from https://www.brainpickings.org/2014/02/18/martin-seligman-gratitude-visit-three-blessings/.

156 **Glassman letter to his mother.** Glassman recorded the exchange, which took place over the Internet, so you can see the emotions that both of them experienced during the call. Transcribed from video: https://www.youtube.com/watch?v=oPuS7SITqgY, accessed July 17, 2016. The other facts and the "almost untouchable" quote are from an interview between Dan and Glassman in July 2016.

157 **Gratitude visit participants still happier one month later.** M. E. P. Seligman, T. A. Steen, N. Park, and C. Peterson (2005). "Positive Psychology Progress: Empirical Validation of Interventions," *American Psychologist* 60: 410–21.

Chapter 8. Multiply Milestones

159 **Couch to 5K.** Dan interviewed Josh Clark in May 2016 and Nancy Griffin (Clark's mom) in July 2016. "The Dreaded W5D3" quote is from a blog post: https://pleasurenotpunishment.wordpress.com/2012/03/17/the-dreaded-w5d3/.

161 **Hundreds of thousands have participated.** The hashtag #c25k on Instagram has been used to tag over 225,000 posts. https://www.instagram.com/explore/tags/c25k/?hl=en, accessed February 10, 2017.

163 **"Freaking Dragons."** Quote is from Steve Kamb (2016). *Level Up Your Life: How to Unlock Adventure and Happiness by Becoming the Hero of Your Own Story*. New York: Rodale, p. 65.

171 **Scott Ettl reads presidential biographies.** Scott Ettl story from interview with Dan in July 2016

173 **Nine million runners in marathons.** Eric J. Allen, Patricia M. Dechow, Devin G. Pope, and George Wu (2014, July). "Reference-Dependent Preferences: Evidence from Marathon Runners," NBER Working Paper No. 20343.

175 **Cal Newport, "obsession with completion."** Cited in blog: https://www.scotthyoung.com/blog/2007/10/18/the-art-of-the-finish-how-to-go-from-busy-to-accomplished/.

Chapter 9: Practice Courage

177 **Nashville sit-ins.** This case study is based on an episode called "Ain't Scared of Your Jails," in the brilliant PBS series *Eyes on the Prize: America's Civil Rights Years* (1995). Most of the series, including this episode, can be found on YouTube. Video footage of Lawson's workshops starts about five minutes into "Ain't Scared of Your Jails." The Taylor Branch quote is from his definitive account of the civil rights movement (1988),

Parting the Waters: America in the King Years 1954–63. New York: Simon & Schuster, p. 286. The arrest figures are from page 290. The Lawson quote about the necessity of "fierce discipline and training" is from a documentary about the history of the strategy of nonviolent action by Steve York, "A Force More Powerful," International Center on Nonviolent Conflict, 1999, https://www.youtube.com/watch?v=_CGlnjfJvHg, accessed March 2, 2017.

182 **Rachman study of bomb-disposal operators.** S. J. Rachman (1982, March). "Development of Courage in Military Personnel in Training and Performance in Combat Situations," U.S. Army Research Report 1338.

183 **Overcoming fear of spiders.** Steps 1, 3, 7, and 9 are from Jayson L. Mystkowski et al. (2006). "Mental Reinstatement of Context and Return of Fear in Spider-Fearful Participants," *Behavior Therapy* 37(1): 49–60. The two-hours statistic is from Katherina K. Hauner et al. (2012). "Exposure Therapy Triggers Lasting Reorganization of Neural Fear Processing," *Proceedings of the National Academy of Sciences* 109(23): 9203–08. The "wouldn't walk on grass for fear of spiders" quote is from http://www.livescience.com/20468-spider-phobia-cured-therapy.html.

186 **Implementation intentions.** Peter M. Gollwitzer (1999). "Implementation Intentions: Strong Effects of Simple Plans," *American Psychologist* 54: 493–503.

187 **Giving voice to values.** Background came from an interview with Dan in June 2010. Quotes from Mary Gentile are from a Q&A on her website: http://www.givingvoicetovaluesthebook.com/about/.

188 **Rabbinical role-play.** The case study is from Paul Vitello (2010, February 10). "Rabbis in Training Receive Lessons in Real-Life Trauma," *New York Times*, http://www.nytimes.com/2010/02/10/nyregion/10acting.html, and Dan's interview in February 2017 with Rabbi Menachem Penner. Thanks to Rabbi Naphtali Lavenda for calling our attention to the story.

190 **Failure of D.A.R.E.** An accessible popular account of the Wei Pan meta-analysis is in http://www.scientificamerican.com/article/why-just-say-no-doesnt-work/. Pim Cuijpers's review (2002) is "Effective Ingredients of School-Based Drug Prevention Programs: A Systematic Review," *Addictive Behaviors* 27: 1012.

191 **Plant a tough question.** A response to an author survey on November 2016.

191 **85% of workers felt unable to raise issue.** Frances J. Milliken (2003). "An Exploratory Study of Employee Silence: Issues That Employees Don't Communicate Upward and Why," http://w4.stern.nyu.edu/emplibrary/Milliken.Frances.pdf.

192 **Brave but Wrong Guy study.** Charlan Nemeth and Cynthia Chiles (1988). "Modelling Courage: The Role of Dissent in Fostering Independence," *European Journal of Social Psychology* 18: 275–80.

197 **Clinic 4: Goldsmith meeting procedure.** Larissa McFarquhar (2009, November 21). "The Better Boss," *New Yorker*.

Chapter 10: Create Shared Meaning

208 **All-hands meeting at Sharp Healthcare.** This story is based on Dan's interviews with Sonia Rhodes in September 2016 and February 2017 and Chip's interviews with Mike Murphy in September 2016 and Lynn Skoczelas in June 2016. Special thanks to Lynn Skoczelas, who organized a half day of focus groups with more than twenty attendees for people inside Sharp to talk with Chip about the Sharp transformation. Further background is in a presentation by Rhodes, "Making Health Care Better: The Story of the Sharp Experience," https://www.oumedicine.com/docs/excel/sharpeexperience--sonia-rhodes-(4-29-11).pdf?sfvrsn=2, accessed March 7, 2017. The "best healthcare system in the universe" quote is from this presentation. The story also uses details from a book by Rhodes and Gary Adamson 2009). *The Complete Guide to Transforming the Patient Experience.* New York: HealthLeaders Media.

210 **Patient satisfaction scores shot up.** The statistics here on patient and physician satisfaction, revenues, etc. were a part of the Baldridge Award application and are also cited in D. G. Lofgren et al. (2007). "Marketing the Health Care Experience: Eight Steps to Infuse Brand Essence into Your Organization," *Health Marketing Quarterly* 23(3): page 121.

212 **Laughter is social.** Provine study description and commentary is from a *Guardian* piece he wrote: https://www.theguardian.com/books/2012/sep/02/why-we-laugh-psychology-provine.

214 **High- and low-ordeal rituals.** Dimitris Xygalatas et al. (2013). "Extreme Rituals Promote Prosociality," *Psychological Science* 24: 1602. How did the researchers know who gave what, if the donations were "anonymous"? They numbered envelopes and questionnaires so they could match the two while maintaining the anonymity of the participants. The result about "high-ordeal observers" is in Ronald Fischer and Dimitris Xygalatas (2014). "Extreme Rituals as Social Technologies," *Journal of Cognition and Culture* 14: 345–55. The result for strangers doing sorting tasks in ice water is in Brock Bastian et al. (2014). "Pain as Social Glue: Shared Pain Increases Cooperation," *Psychological Science* 25(11): 2079–85.

217 **Purpose/Passion.** Hansen's purpose/passion material is from an early draft of his forthcoming book *Great at Work: How Top Performers Work Less and Achieve More.*

218 **"magical entity . . . waiting to be discovered."** This Wrzesniewski quote is from Angela Duckworth (2016). *Grit: The Power of Passion and Perseverance.* New York: Scribner, p. 153.

219 **Lifeguard study.** Adam M. Grant (2008). "The Significance of Task Significance: Job Performance Effects, Relational Mechanisms, and Boundary Conditions," *Journal of Applied Psychology* 93(1): 108–24.

220 **Nurses and radiologists.** Adam M. Grant (2014), in Morten Ann Gernsbacher, ed., *Psychology and the Real World,* 2nd ed. New York: Worth.

221 **Hospital janitor combatting patient loneliness.** Amy Wrzesniewski, Nicholas LoBuglio, Jane E. Dutton, and Justin M. Berg (2013). "Job-Crafting and Cultivating Positive Meaning and Identity in Work," *Advances in Positive Organizational Psychology* 1: 281–302.

221 **Sharp baby shower.** This story is from a group interview by Chip in June 2016 that Baehrens attended.

Chapter 11: Deepen Ties

223 **Turnaround at Stanton Elementary.** Stanton story drawn from Dan's interviews in January 2016 with Susan Stevenson, Carlie John Fisherow, Melissa Bryant, and Anna Gregory at District of Columbia Public Schools (DCPS). Also documents provided by Stevenson. Suspension and truancy

data provided by Flamboyan Foundation and verified by Anna Gregory at DCPS. DCPS provided the definition of truancy. The performance data for subsequent years were in documents by Flamboyan, verified by either Fisherow or DCPS. In particular, reading and math scores are from DCPS: https://assets.documentcloud.org/documents/1238775/2014-dc-cas-scores-by-school.pdf.

231 **Responsiveness.** H. T. Reis (2007). "Steps Toward the Ripening of Relationship Science," *Personal Relationships* 14: 1–23. This paper arose when Reis won a "distinguished scholar" award from a psychological society for researchers who are studying close relationships. This kind of recognition gave him a platform at a professional conference to make a case to his fellow researchers about where the research should go, and this paper is his answer.

233 **Healthier diurnal cortisol.** Finding is from http://www.ncbi.nlm.nih.gov/pubmed/26015413.

233 **Gallup's six most revealing questions.** Marcus Buckingham and Curt Coffman (1999). *First Break All the Rules.* New York: Simon & Schuster.

235 **Bisognano's younger brother, Johnny.** Bisognano's story from interview with Dan in August 2016 unless otherwise noted. The "they'd speak over him" and "I'm not gonna make it" quotes are from http://theconversation-project.org/about/maureen-bisognano/. The "What matters to you?" question is from Michael J. Barry and Susan Edgman-Levitan (2012). "Shared Decision Making—The Pinnacle of Patient-Centered Care," *New England Journal of Medicine* 366 : 780–81. Full disclosure: After we wrote about another aspect of the IHI's work in a prior book, *Switch*, Dan was invited to give several paid keynotes for the IHI, which is how he met Maureen Bisognano and learned about this story.

236 **Kendra had autism.** This story from Dan's conversation with Jen Rodgers in February 2017.

240 **"Baggage" handling at call centers.** Baggage handling data from research document provided by the Corporate Executive Board. Context from Dan's call with Matt Dixon and Eric Braun in August 2016.

242 **Bus stop high/low intimacy conversations.** Z. Rubin (1974). "Lovers

and Other Strangers: The Development of Intimacy in Encounters and Relationships: Experimental studies of self-disclosure between strangers at bus stops and in airport departure lounges can provide clues about the development of intimate relationships," *American Scientist* 62(2): 182–90.

243 **Art Aron 36 questions.** A. Aron et al. (1997). "The Experimental Generation of Interpersonal Closeness: A Procedure and Some Preliminary Findings," *Personality and Social Psychology Bulletin* 23: 363–77.

245 **Mike Elam office conversation.** From survey response from Elam in March 2016 and subsequent email exchange in August 2016.

249 **Clinic 5: How Can You Combat the "Silo" Mentality?** The Pit Crew experience is not made up—you can hire a vendor to bring the experience to your off-site. Dan has seen it and it's pretty neat. See more at http://www.bobparker.ca/pitcrewblog/. The "crucial conversations" phrase is based on a popular and useful book by Kerry Patterson, Joseph Grenny, Ron McMillan, and Al Switzler (2002). *Crucial Conversations: Tools for Talking When Stakes Are High.* New York: McGraw-Hill Education.

Chapter 12: Making Moments Matter

254 **MIT acceptance packet.** http://toastable.com/2010/lets-get-personal/.

256 **Regrets of the dying.** http://www.bronnieware.com/regrets-of-the-dying/.

258 **Julie Kasten.** From Dan's interview with Julie Kasten in June 2015.

260 **Suresh Mistry, Warren and Betsy Talbot, and Nancy Schaufele.** Stories were collected August–September 2016 after a newsletter was sent out in early August 2016.

264 **Wendy sees snow.** Story drawn from Dan's interviews with Darcy Daniels, Jessica Marsh, and Cori Fogarty in October 2016 and Darcy's blog post https://bravefragilewarriors.wordpress.com/2016/04/03/snow-day-in-the-hospital/.

Index

About the Authors

The Heath brothers have written three *New York Times* bestselling books: *Made to Stick*, *Switch* and *Decisive*. Their books have sold over two million copies worldwide and have been translated into thirty-three languages including Thai, Arabic and Lithuanian.

Chip Heath is a professor at the Stanford Graduate School of Business, teaching courses on strategy and organizations. He has helped more than 450 start-ups hone their business strategy and messages. He lives in Los Gatos, California.

Dan Heath is a senior fellow at Duke University's CASE Center, which supports entrepreneurs fighting for social good. He lives in Durham, North Carolina.